MELTING
POT

MELTING POT

Stories and Recipes from a
Chinese American Daydreamer

SAMANTHA MUI

PHOTOGRAPHS BY HANNAH MENDENHALL SCHMUCK

Published by Samantha Mui

Publisher's Cataloging-In-Publication Data
(Prepared by The Donohue Group, Inc.)

Names: Mui, Samantha, author. | Schmuck, Hannah Mendenhall, photographer.
Title: Melting pot : stories and recipes from a Chinese American daydreamer / Samantha Mui ; photography by Hannah Mendenhall Schmuck.
Description: First edition. | [East Palo Alto, California] : Samantha Mui, [2020] | Includes index.
Identifiers: ISBN 9780578662619 | ISBN 9780578662626 (ebook)
Subjects: LCSH: International cooking. | Cooking, Chinese. | Cooking, American. | Cooking, Asian. | Cooking, European. | Mui, Samantha--Childhood and youth. | LCGFT: Cookbooks.
Classification: LCC TX724.5.A1 M85 2020 (print) | LCC TX724.5.A1 (ebook) | DDC 641.59--dc23

ISBN 978-0-578-66261-9
eBook ISBN 978-0-578-66262-6

Recipes and Stories: Samantha Mui
Developmental Editor: Julianne Bigler
Copy Chief: Gail O'Hara
Recipe Editor: Kelsey Vala

Photographs by Hannah Mendenhall Schmuck, except for page 10 by Hieu Tran, and page 14 and 237 by Kwan Chan

Book design by Hannah Mendenhall Schmuck
www.hannahrms.com

First Edition

This book is dedicated to all the dreamers and doers around the world, those who wake up every day inspired to make a difference. No matter what adversities we face, we will continue running our own race as fearlessly and graciously as possible!

CONTENTS

Chapter One

ONE-POT WONDER

16

Chapter Two

COOKIE CLOG

32

Chapter Three

WOULDN'T MISS IT

48

INTRODUCTION

Ever since I was a kid, I have always loved stories and food. My mom (Joanna Mui) would drop me off at the library for two hours and I would curl up in a corner with piles of picture books about food. I watched cooking shows while other kids were watching cartoons. Those shows piqued my interest about how other people lived and gave me a strong urge to connect with others through food. Food was at the center of all my family gatherings, and it became the center of my life and activities.

As a Chinese-American latchkey kid growing up in the Bay Area, I was very much aware of both the Chinese and U.S. cultural norms that made me feel inadequate. But eventually I overcame my insecurity, body shame and feelings of not being Chinese enough or American enough and accepted my authentic self. Cooking was a way to bring joy into my life, celebrate every day with my favorite people and even a form of therapy.

When I started culinary school, I realized that I had already learned so much from my frugal/resourceful grandmothers, exotic family friends and my culture. The comfort I had found in other people's homes, the exposure to other cultures and cuisines and the curiosity to experiment with creativity in the kitchen had all contributed to helping me become the person and cook that I am.

While culinary school helped spark my creative style, I don't make a fuss about having perfect technique. This book is about sharing my story, the comforting dishes inspired by my upbringing and the joy of making delicious and easy meals. I hope my story and my food will inspire you to find your own creative flair in the kitchen, eventually freeing you from following recipes and rules. Most of the recipes in this book are simple, and I've added my own twist on comfort foods from my culinary background.

In addition to wanting to make cooking enjoyable, I hope my versatile recipes and essays will inspire you to be authentic and find your own niche in life. Life is about second chances and finding your own story.

With a heart full of gratitude (and always a full stomach),

FOOD
PHILOSOPHY

FOOD CONNECTS PEOPLE

Food can be a powerful vehicle for bringing people together. It has the power to bring back nostalgic memories and create lasting new ones.

MASTER COOKING TECHNIQUES, NOT RECIPES

I've always had a hard time sticking to rules, and I couldn't understand why I had to follow everything. In my early life, this caused a lot of frustration when I tried to break free from the confines of structure. It wasn't until I went to culinary school that I learned that having a foundation is important. Sometimes when I am creating a recipe, it comes from a classic dish that I enjoy. In my head, I dissect what I like and dislike, then work my way backward to achieve a pleasing result.

BALANCE OVER MEASURE

There are three components to balance in food: flavor, texture and presentation. I learned early on from my paternal grandmother (Rosanna Mui, a.k.a. 嫲嫲, a.k.a. Mama) that our taste buds can detect five main flavors: sweet, sour, bitter, salty and spicy. For her, and many of the women in my life, there was no need to follow recipes because the goal was creating balance. She followed her taste buds, not recipes. Texture isn't something we always consider when creating a dish. One way to immediately elevate a dish is by adding a contrasting texture. For example, if you have a soft meat loaf, serve it with a crunchy roasted vegetable. The last step in creating a meal is finding balance in ratios and contrasting colors for visual appeal.

In my childhood kitchen, each tool had many functions: a cleaver could be a fish knife, meat cutter and garlic press all in one. Watching my grandma save all the packets of BBQ sauce and ketchup at fast-food joints taught me that each bit counts. Leftover salad dressing or sauce can be used as a marinade for meat or other proteins. Leftover vegetables, a small garlic clove, a chicken carcass and a bit of pasta could all be used to make a soup. Having limitations can be a launching pad for creativity.

HAVE A GAME PLAN

Whether you're cooking for one or for the masses, success is all in the prep work. I'm not ashamed to use many quality premade products to create the meal I want in the time I have. Write a list of what needs to be done so you can easily see what needs to be started first. For example, if you're making a roast dinner, get the roast in before you peel potatoes and vegetables or make the sides. For larger feasts, chop vegetables the day before, put them into plastic bags and keep premade sauces in a jar. The big day should be more about assembling, not cooking. Ultimately, food is meant to be enjoyed—and you shouldn't have to feel like a prisoner in your own kitchen.

Chapter One

ONE-POT WONDER

Soy Sauce Eggs

Garlic Bok Choy

Hapa Fried Rice

Chicken & Rice

Mama's Oxtail

Sweet Red Bean Soup

There's a word in Cantonese called *wei sick* (為食), which describes a person who is always hungry and looking for something to eat. I have fit that description since I came out of my mother's womb at 9 pounds, 4 ounces, eating six meals a day as a child. Far from being a picky eater with a grimace on my face, I awaited meals with utensils in hand. I looked forward to what I might munch on between meals.

My mother, however, is the opposite of wei sick. She eats primarily for nourishment, not enjoyment. Not only is she an abstemious eater, cooking is a mundane chore for her. When I was a child, she stuck to a small sample of staple foods that require little effort to prepare. This presented a problem for her wei sick daughter. Upon opening the fridge looking for a treat, I could be sure to find cabbage, carrots, minced pork, thawing chicken drumsticks and something no Chinese kitchen would be complete without: ginger.

I never knew what would be served at the dinner table, as my mom's go-to dishes were an assortment of ingredients she chopped and tossed into a hot pot or wok until it looked ready. We never knew what to expect in mom's "one-pot wonders," only their frequency. These dinners taught me a few things at a young age: I could expect the unexpected, there was only one way to prepare chicken and that I needed more options.

My mother now jokes that I should thank her for her one-pot wonders: If it hadn't been for these surprise stews, my passion for cooking may never have been ignited, proving just how wei sick I actually was. The recipes that follow remind me of my mom's cooking style.

SOY SAUCE EGGS

If you were to ever peek into my mother's fridge, you would find the following things: knobs of ginger, garlic, tofu, chicken drumsticks and always eggs. My mom would sneak an egg into every meal. Eggs always took but a minute to prepare, and these soy sauce eggs are no different.

SERVES 4

6 eggs

3 pieces rock sugar or 3 tablespoons sugar

½ cup low-sodium soy sauce

1 tablespoon unseasoned rice wine vinegar

1 cup water

1 whole star anise

1   Place eggs in a small pot and cover with water. Bring pot to a boil, and boil eggs for 7 minutes. Next, submerge the boiled eggs under cold water by transferring them with a slotted spoon to a bowl with ice water. Once cooled, peel the eggs.

2   In a small pot, combine the rest of ingredients. Bring to a simmer and add the peeled eggs. Simmer eggs for an additional 7 minutes. Transfer eggs with the liquid into an airtight container and refrigerate for at least 6 hours or overnight. Serve as an appetizer or with rice and meat.

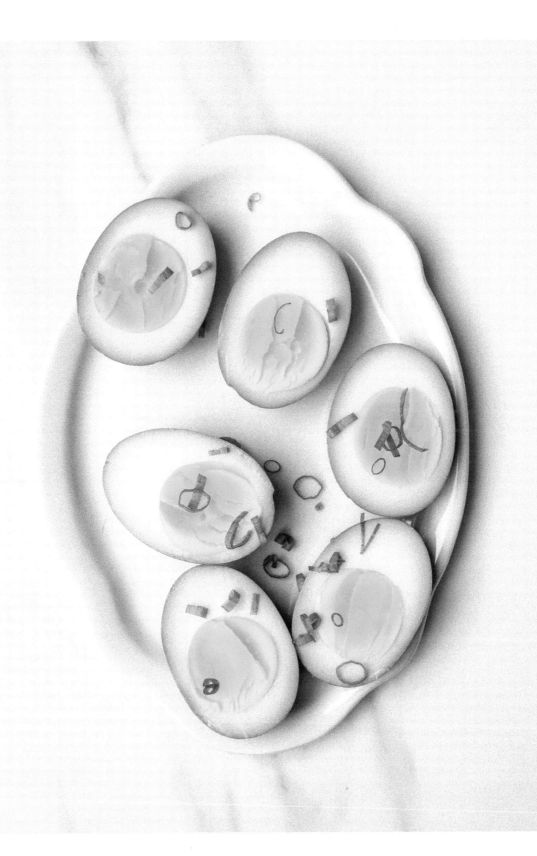

GARLIC BOK CHOY

My mom loved to make bok choy when I was young. She was the only one in the family who liked it, and I would watch her savor each crunchy leaf. The way she chomped the leaves always enticed me, though I didn't like it as a youngster. I'm glad I've inherited her taste as an adult. Slurp away!

SERVES 2

2 heads bok choy

2 tablespoons garlic, minced

1 tablespoon ginger, peeled and cut into fine strips

2 tablespoons vegetable or canola oil

1   Trim the base of the bok choy to separate the leaves. Discard the base and lightly wash the bok choy in cold water. Pat dry.

2   Heat oil in a wok or large pan over medium-high heat. Add garlic and ginger and cook until golden and fragrant. Be careful not to burn the mixture. Add bok choy stems to the skillet. Cook for 3 to 5 minutes until slightly tender.

HAPA FRIED RICE

My mom isn't the type of woman to let a lack of ingredients stop her from getting dinner on the table. She often used leftovers to whip up many variations of this dish. I've tried this so many different ways, I can now say that there are no rules. While the suggested ingredients are merely a guideline, the directions matter. This recipe is great for the more fastidious palate, as you may choose any vegetables you desire. The sky is the limit!

SERVES 4

1 whole fresh pineapple

3 tablespoons sesame oil, divided

4 eggs, beaten

3 garlic cloves, minced

2 tablespoons scallions, thinly sliced

1 cup of sausages or ham, cut into
  small cubes

½ cup chopped pineapple
  (canned or fresh)

3 cups cooked leftover jasmine rice

1 tablespoon soy sauce

¼ teaspoon salt

1 To make 2 pineapple boats for the fried rice, with the leaves attached to the pineapple, slice in half lengthwise, and using a small paring knife, cut the flesh around the edge of pineapple leaving about ¾-inch of flesh attached to the skin. Begin removing small chunks of the fruit from the boat. Scrape the bottom of the pineapple boat with a spoon to smooth it out. Reserve half a cup of the fruit and chop into ½-inch pieces. Store the rest of the fruit for later use. Cover pineapple boats and set aside.

2 Heat 1 tablespoon sesame oil in a wok over medium heat. Add beaten eggs and turn heat to medium-low. Cook until soft and slightly wet. Set aside.

3 Using the same pan, pour 2 tablespoons sesame oil and add garlic, 1 tablespoon of scallions, apple sausages and chopped pineapples. Cook until caramelized. Add the rice and egg, mixed thoroughly, leaving small chunks of eggs in the rice. Add soy sauce, remainder of sesame oil and salt, and mix thoroughly. Spoon fried rice into the pineapple bowls, and garnish with the remaining scallions.

CHICKEN & RICE

There's no chicken recipe quite like this one. This dish showcases my experience with cooking Chinese food: nothing gets discarded. For this recipe, the poaching liquid is used in the rice, and as a base for a yummy soup.

SERVES 4

CHICKEN

4 chicken thighs with skin and bone intact (about 1½ pounds)

1 tablespoon salt

3 scallions, cut in half

3-4 slices of ginger, no need to peel

½ onion

3 garlic cloves, minced

1 tablespoon sesame oil

Handful of cilantro, for garnish

Cucumbers slices and tomatoes, for garnish

Sambal (optional)

1 For the chicken, rub the salt, scallions and ginger into the chicken. Place in a large pot or stockpot. Add onion and garlic into the pot. Fill pot with enough water (about 2.5 quarts) to cover chicken by about an inch and bring to a gentle boil over medium heat. Simmer for 8 to 10 minutes. Turn the heat off and place a tight-fitting lid on the pot. Allow chicken thighs to sit in the pot covered for 30 minutes.

2 Meanwhile, fill a large bowl with ice water. Remove thighs from pot and check that the internal temperature reaches 165°F. If not, return to pot for a few minutes more. Place thighs into the cold water and let sit for 2 to 3 minutes. Remove chicken from water, and drizzle with sesame oil and set aside. Season chicken broth to taste with salt, and reserve for making the rice and as a side of soup.

2 tablespoons garlic, minced

1 tablespoon ginger, minced

1 tablespoon vegetable oil

2 cups jasmine rice, washed

Reserved chicken broth

3 To cook the rice in a rice cooker, heat oil over medium heat in a sauté pan or wok. Add garlic and ginger. Cook until fragrant. Add washed rice and stir until fully mixed and the rice kernel is slightly toasted. Transfer rice mixture into a rice cooker. Pour reserve chicken broth into rice cooker. (Amount may vary according to individual rice cooker.) To cook the rice on the stovetop, heat oil over medium heat. Add garlic and ginger. Cook until fragrant. Then add washed rice in a medium pot, stir until fully mixed and rice kernels are slightly toasted. Next, add 4 cups of the reserved chicken broth and bring to boil. Once it boils, immediately cover the pot and turn the heat to a low setting and cook for another 15 minutes. Take it off the heat and fluff the rice kernels with a fork.

2 tablespoons ginger, minced

4 scallions, minced

1 red chili pepper, minced

¼ cup oil

½ teaspoon sugar

1 teaspoon salt

4 For the oil, mix ginger, scallions and chili peppers in a heatproof bowl. Heat oil in microwave for 1 minute, then pour on top of the other ingredients. Mix in sugar and salt. Let mixture cool to room temperature.

Serve chicken with rice, a drizzle of ginger scallion oil, cucumber slices and cilantro. Serve the reserved chicken broth as a side to accompany the meal.

MAMA'S OXTAIL

Although I lovingly tease my mom about her cooking, there are a few dishes that she does fabulously. I can't tell you how many times she burned a pot while making stew. Thankfully, the pressure cooker has come to her rescue in recent years, so she can just set it and forget it. After hours of slow cooking, this oxtail melts in your mouth. Any red wine will do for the braising liquid. Best served over a bed of freshly cooked white rice.

SERVES 2

3 tablespoons vegetable oil

1 pound oxtails

3 whole garlic cloves

2 tablespoons sliced ginger

½ onion, sliced

½ cup red wine

¼ cup soy sauce

2–3 pieces rock sugar or 2 tablespoons
   granulated sugar

2 cups beef broth

2 star anise pods

Jasmine rice, cooked, for serving

Salt and black pepper

1   Season the oxtail with salt and black pepper. Heat the oil in a large skillet over medium-high heat, then add the oxtails. Sear oxtails on both top and bottom and around the meat. If you use an Instant Pot, you can sear the oxtails directly in the Instant Pot using the sauté function. Once caramelized, set the meat aside. Leave rendered fat in the skillet or Instant Pot, and add garlic, ginger and onions. Sauté mixture until caramelized, and deglaze with wine, scraping up any browned bits in the bottom of the skillet. Simmer for 1 to 2 minutes to allow the wine to reduce slightly. Add soy sauce, rock sugar, beef broth and star anise.

2   Add the oxtails and sauce to the pressure cooker or add the oxtails back to the Instant Pot. Pressure-cook oxtails for 45 minutes, then Natural Release for another 20 minutes, following the instructions for using the Instant Pot or pressure cooker. To test for readiness of oxtails, insert a toothpick into the meat closest to the bone. If it slides effortlessly into the meat, it is ready. Serve on a bed of rice.

SWEET RED BEAN SOUP

My mom's favorite thing to make was soup. She swore that Chinese soups were her secret for staying youthful. This warm dessert soup is usually eaten after a meal. Bonus: the adzuki bean used in this recipe is a superfood.

SERVES 6

1 cup adzuki red beans, found in many Asian markets

2 tablespoons mini tapioca pearls

10 cups water

½ teaspoon orange zest

2 knobs rock sugar or 2 tablespoons brown sugar

1 cup sweetened coconut milk, plus more to taste

1   In a bowl, cover adzuki red beans with 2 inches of water and soak overnight.

2   The next day, in a large pot, bring beans and 10 cups of water to a boil, then cook on medium-high heat for 1 hour. Add water to thin out the mixture, if needed.

3   Meanwhile, in a small saucepan, bring enough water to a boil to submerge the tapioca pearls. Add tapioca pearls and simmer for 8 to 10 minutes until they become translucent. Using a slotted spoon, transfer tapioca pearls to a bowl with ice water.

4   When beans are cooked, add orange zest, sugar and sweetened coconut milk to the pot. Fold tapioca pearls into beans. Simmer all together for 5 minutes. Serve this dessert hot, and drizzle each serving with coconut milk, to taste.

COOKIE CLOG

You might have known someone like the person I was in grade school. I was the girl staring out the window, asking for the question to be repeated after being jolted back to reality from my daydreams. Maybe you were like me. Having moved to a new school in fourth grade, I might have been a Judy Blume heroine as the new girl wearing hand-me-downs. I was a latchkey kid lost in her fantasies, known for being "ditzy and too bubbly."

Mental escapism was not just my default but my haven from bullying. My Lutheran mother had taught me to "turn the other cheek," and I sometimes laughed along with the girls who laughed at me, hoping to befriend them.

Many days in grade school were spent at home alone being "sick." Daytime TV exposed me to a whole world my conservative background had sheltered me from. I watched everything from paternity talk shows to *7th Heaven*, fascinated by the diversity of people's lives—whether they were realistic or not.

These sick days also introduced me to the original food stars such as Lidia Bastianich, Martha Stewart and Nigella Lawson. I was shocked that chicken wasn't only used in stews but could be fried, roasted, breaded or boiled. In my small apartment kitchen, I would pretend I was the star of my own food show, cooking the dishes I saw with a whisk and empty mixing bowl and reciting lines from the hosts. I pretended to cook with the few utensils we owned. Every Chinese household is guaranteed to have a cleaver, wok and chopsticks, but we didn't have other basic utensils such as measuring cups or spoons. In fact, none of the women in my life measured their ingredients. They seemed to be guided by an intuition for precisely the right measurements for a perfect recipe. Having supplies only honed my skills for improvisation.

At age eight, I attempted my first recipe from a food show, which I like to call "Failed Peanut Butter Cookies." I would learn later is that cooking is an art and baking is a science—the latter doesn't take well to improvising. My version of precision was eyeballing the measurements, kneading the cookie dough like bread dough, then plopping the dollops closely together on an ungreased cookie sheet and shoving it into a toaster oven.

Within five minutes, I detected the smell of burning sugar. My eyes widened when I saw the "cookies" that had baked into a gooey mass and were leaking under the burners. I turned the toaster oven off immediately and tried to get rid of the evidence: cramming the sludge into the sink until it clogged. I felt panicked and ashamed. A cookie recipe and a broken sink—would I ever be allowed to stay home again? In my peril, I called my grandmother (Popo) and uncle, who came to my rescue. With a flick of a switch and some dough-pushing, the sludge slowly disappeared. After apologizing, I pleaded with them to not tell my parents about the catastrophe. I cleaned up the kitchen before my parents came home and had many more days of failed attempts at cooking.

It took a few years before I finally made a few edible dishes. To this day, I'm still haunted by baking. I am more of a freestyle cook who prefers dishes that provide for some leeway and personal style. If I do bake, I have been known to use a premade mix, but I'll still add my own spin on it.

COCONUT MACAROONS

These are the type of cookies I'll make when I have to make a bunch of cookies in a snap. This recipe is simple and you don't have to slave over the perfect shape. My favorite part is the sweet, chewy, slightly burnt coconut bits that flake off the pan at the end.

MAKES 24 COOKIES

32 ounces unsweetened coconut flakes

1 (14-ounce) can sweetened
   condensed milk

1 teaspoon vanilla extract

1   Preheat oven to 325°F.

2   Mix all ingredients together in a large bowl.

3   Using two spoons, scoop out equal portions of the coconut mixture, and drop onto a lined cookie sheet, about 2 tablespoons per cookie. Bake for 12 minutes.

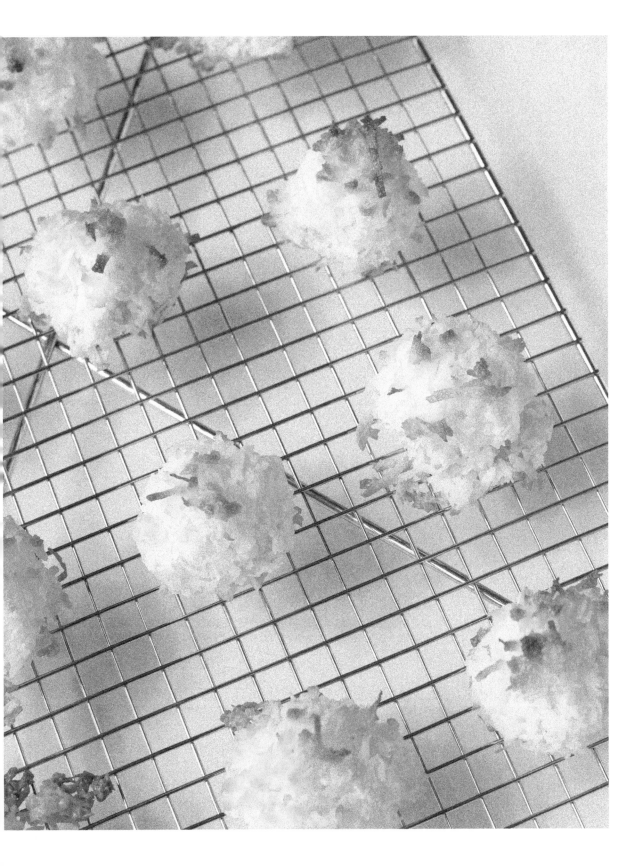

PEANUT BUTTER & JAM COOKIES

You'll never forget your first batch of cookies. While my experience was more dramatic than average, it's not in my nature to give up after the first try. However, to avoid getting burned in the kitchen these days, I prefer to stick to very simple recipes. The raspberry-filled center is a unique and delectable addition.

MAKES 12 COOKIES

1 cup brown sugar

1 cup smooth peanut butter

1 egg

1 teaspoon vanilla extract

3 tablespoons raspberry jam

1   Preheat oven to 350°F. Combine all ingredients except the jam in a medium-size bowl until smooth and blended. Chill dough in fridge for at least one hour.

2   Roll out 12 equal-size balls of dough and place them two inches apart on a greased and lined cookie sheet. With the back of a wooden spoon, make a small dimple in the center of each cookie, and add ¼ teaspoon of jam into the center. Bake for 10 minutes, until edges of cookies appear to be set. Let cookies cool for 10 minutes before serving.

EVERYTHING BUT
THE KITCHEN SINK COOKIES

It's never fun to begin baking only to find you're lacking one key ingredient. You could ask your neighbor for it, or you could try this snappy recipe. All you need is premade cookie dough and some type of crushed snack food that is probably sitting in your cabinets right now. Chocolate chips, pretzels, graham crackers, potato chips... what's your pleasure?

MAKES 14 LARGE COOKIES

2 (16-ounce) packages chocolate-chip cookie dough

2 cups toppings mixture (smashed potato chips, pretzel sticks, toffee bits, granola bits, chopped caramels, chopped walnuts, etc.)

1 Preheat oven to 350°F. In a bowl, mix half of smashed ingredients into cookie dough. Scoop out 14 large balls onto a greased and lined cookie sheet, leaving at least two inches of space between each ball. Press toppings onto each ball.

2 Let dough chill in the fridge for at least 30 minutes. Bake for 15 minutes or until cookies are golden brown.

CANDIED BACON
STOVE-TOP S'MORES

Why wait for camp to have s'mores? Get the fixings, and you can have toasty warm s'mores in your kitchen any time. This recipe adds another level to the traditional s'more: candied bacon. As if crumbly graham crackers, gooey marshmallows and chocolate don't already do the trick, try it with a fat component. Everyone will want one...

MAKES 4 S'MORES

CANDIED BACON

4 strips bacon

2 tablespoons brown sugar

⅛ teaspoon cracked black pepper

S'MORES

4 graham crackers

4 marshmallows

4 large pieces dark chocolate
  (2 ounces each)

1   Preheat oven to 325°F. Lay bacon on parchment paper–lined baking sheet. Sprinkle black pepper and brown sugar on front and back of each strip, rubbing evenly. Bake for 25 to 30 minutes. Flip strips over halfway through baking for even cooking. Remove from oven and let cool slightly.

2   Lay out graham crackers on a plate and break each one in half. Place 1 strip of candied bacon and a piece of chocolate on one half of each cracker.

3   Turn on stove-top heat to medium. Apply one marshmallow to a skewer. Place the marshmallow close to, but not touching, the flame, and roast until it is brown and bubbly on all sides. Place the marshmallow onto the chocolate and top with the other graham cracker half. Repeat with remaining marshmallows.

CHOCOLATE TOFU MOUSSE

Tofu was a staple in my household growing up, but I wasn't a fan at the time. I had only eaten it cooked and served with savory foods. However, tofu is truly a versatile food that will absorb any flavor you give it. This tofu pudding has a silky texture and can satisfy a sweet tooth.

SERVES 2

½ cup dark chocolate chips

1 teaspoon vanilla extract

1 16-ounce package silken tofu

3 tablespoons honey

1   In a small microwave-safe bowl, melt chocolate in microwave in 30-second increments. Add vanilla extract and cool for 5 minutes.

2   In a blender, blend tofu, honey and chocolate mixture until smooth. Place in glass cups and refrigerate for at least an hour to allow the mixture to firm.

3   Garnish with fresh raspberries, chocolate shavings, dried coconut or mint leaves.

STOVE-TOP CRISP

This crisp is every bit as delicious as a baked one but takes less work. The granola topping holds its shape better than oats and makes the top extra crispy.

SERVES 2

4 tablespoons brown sugar, divided

4 tablespoons butter, divided

1 cup granola

2 cups nectarines, sliced or cubed

¼ teaspoon cinnamon

1 teaspoon vanilla extract

1 tablespoon lemon juice

1 teaspoon cornstarch

2 scoops vanilla ice cream

1   In a small pan on medium heat, melt 2 tablespoons brown sugar in 2 tablespoons butter for 1 minute. Reduce heat to medium-low and add granola. Stir constantly until golden brown. Place in a bowl and set aside.

2   In the same pan on medium-low heat, add remaining butter and brown sugar, and cook nectarines until slightly tender. Add cinnamon, vanilla extract, lemon juice and cornstarch. Stir to dissolve cornstarch. Cook until fruit is soft, then remove heat and let cool for 5 minutes.

3   Sprinkle the crumble onto the fruit and serve with a scoop of ice cream.

Chapter Three

WOULDN'T MISS IT

Mochi Rice Waffles

Creamy Tomato Soup

Cheesy Bread

Pastry Pockets

Baked Bolognese

Layered Lasagna

Childhood is perhaps the most authentic period of our lives, when who we are has not been tamed into our tempered selves. My appetite for celebration has long been what drives me, even when I was a naive child committing social faux pas. As a child I craved the excitement of anything that hinted at a party, so much so that by the fourth grade I planned my own birthdays, buying my own invitations and asking my mom to drive me to the store for party decorations.

When I was about five, my neighbors threw a birthday party for one of their children who was around my age. Birthday decor spilled out on to their lawn as though the circus had come to town. Seeing the festivities, I hastily asked my mother for permission to go and raced across the street with my older brother, Samuel. Their mother opened the door and we quickly threw our shoes on to a pile of others and bolted inside.

Dozens of kids were scattered everywhere, waiting their turn in line for games that spotted the entire house. Toward the end of the party, the children gathered together to claim their goody bags. Each child received a personalized bag with their name printed on it. After most of them had received their bag, I boldly raised my hand and asked for mine. The woman handing them out looked through the remaining bags in confusion. She exchanged whispers with the hostess about the missing bags, and I heard, "They weren't invited." Instead of receiving a colorful, handwritten goody bag like the others, I got a bag hastily assembled with leftover treats and cheap plastic toys.

It wasn't until several years later while reading my vocabulary list at school that I understood what it meant to be "invited." The circumstances of the joyous occasion years before dawned on me. Maybe I should have felt embarrassed, but I look back and see a kid who just wanted to be in the midst of every celebration under the sun. I wouldn't have missed it for the world.

The following recipes were inspired by some of my favorite childhood foods.

MOCHI RICE WAFFLES

One of my fondest memories about food involves waffles. My mom made waffles for my brother and me on the weekends with an iron that imprinted the letters of the alphabet all on a grid. This recipe calls for rice flour, which makes the texture chewier than traditional fluffy American waffles.

SERVES 4

¾ cup rice flour

¼ cup all-purpose flour

1 teaspoon baking powder

¼ teaspoon salt

1 egg

1 cup coconut milk

¼ cup sweetened condensed milk

3 tablespoons butter, melted

1   Preheat your waffle iron.

2   Mix all dry ingredients in a bowl. In a separate bowl, mix the wet ingredients. Slowly mix dry ingredients into the wet ingredients, stirring until fully combined.

3   Cook the waffles on the preheated waffle iron; the amount of batter will depend on the type of iron. Serve hot with honey or desired fruit toppings.

CREAMY TOMATO SOUP

I am obsessed with a good creamy tomato soup. The thing I love about it is that it's simple enough to make for yourself any night of the week, and if garnished right, can be elevated to a dinner-party food.

SERVES 4

4 tablespoons unsalted butter

1 large onion, chopped

1 (28-ounce) can whole peeled tomatoes

4–6 whole basil leaves

⅓ cup Parmesan cheese, grated

1 tablespoon balsamic vinegar

1½ cups room-temperature half-and-half

1 teaspoon sugar

½ teaspoon fine sea salt

Cracked black pepper

1   On medium heat, sweat onions in butter until translucent. Be careful not to burn. Add tomatoes, basil leaves, Parmesan cheese, balsamic vinegar, half-and-half and sugar. Simmer for 5 minutes.

2   Puree the soup in a blender until smooth. Season with salt and pepper, to taste. Serve with fresh basil leaves and a drizzle of olive oil.

CHEESY BREAD

This comforting cheesy bread is reminiscent of those crispy squares you can't stop munching on. The blend of cheddar and Parmesan cheese creates a rich flavor for this hearty snack.

SERVES 6

¼ cup mayonnaise

3 tablespoons butter, softened

3 cloves garlic, minced

2 cups shredded cheddar cheese

1 cup shredded Parmesan cheese

1 large, oval loaf French bread, cut in half lengthwise

Cracked black pepper

1   Set oven to broil. In a bowl, mix mayo, butter, garlic and cheeses. Spread mixture evenly onto the cut halves of the bread. Season with black pepper.

2   Place bread on a baking sheet, cheesy halves facing up, and broil for 5 to 6 minutes, until cheese is melted and bubbly. Remove bread and let sit for 5 minutes. Cut into slices and serve.

PASTRY POCKETS

In elementary school, my brother and I were obsessed with eating frozen Hot Pockets. Just two minutes in the microwave and out came this savory, carb-loaded snack. We ate them whole in just a few minutes, despite them being scorching hot. This homemade Hot Pockets recipe is an homage to our beloved childhood meal. You can also prepare ahead of time and keep frozen until serving.

MAKES 8 HOT POCKETS

1 17.3-ounce box puff pastry dough with 2 sheets, thawed

1 egg, beaten

3 tablespoons water

FILLING

1 cup cooked sausage crumbles

½ cup cheddar or mozzarella cheese

Cracked black pepper

1   Preheat oven to 400°F. Place the two sheets of puff pastry dough onto a lightly floured surface. Cut each sheet into 4 rectangles and lightly roll it using a rolling pin. Add the filling onto one side of the rectangle, leaving ½-inch space around the edges. Fold pastry in half to seal the filling, then crimp edges all the way around using fork prongs.

2   Cut a few slits on top of the pocket and brush with beaten egg and water. Sprinkle with a thin layer of cheese. Bake pockets on a cookie sheet for 18 to 20 minutes until golden and flaky.

PULLED PORK AND CHEDDAR CHEESE

1 cup pulled pork

½ cup cheddar cheese

2 tablespoons green
  onions, chopped

PIZZA FLAVORED

1 cup mozzarella cheese

½ cup pizza sauce

½ cup chopped pepperoni

CHEDDAR AND BROCCOLI

1 cup cheddar cheese

1 cup chopped sautéed broccoli

1 minced garlic clove

Salt and pepper to taste

HAM AND EGGS

1 cup scrambled eggs

½ cup chopped ham

Salt and pepper to taste

CHORIZO AND EGGS

1 cup scrambled eggs

½ cup cooked chorizo

¼ cup cheddar cheese

FETA AND SPINACH

½ pound sautéed spinach

1 cup crumbled feta

1 teaspoon lemon zest

Salt and pepper to taste

BAKED BOLOGNESE

This Bolognese sauce is very forgiving, so whether you're an experienced cook or not, you'll have a delicious dinner on your hands. I like to bake this dish in a round pan. The first slice of this pasta will make you feel like it's your birthday every night of the week.

SERVES 6

1 pound spaghetti

2 tablespoons olive oil, plus more for greasing pan

⅓ cup celery, finely chopped

⅓ cup carrots, finely chopped

½ cup onions, finely chopped

½ pound ground pork

½ pound ground beef

¼ cup red wine

1 pound canned whole Roma tomatoes

¼ cup whole milk

1 egg

½ cup shredded Parmesan cheese

Salt and black pepper

1   Bring large pot of water with salt to a boil. Cook spaghetti until al dente. Drain and set aside in a large bowl, toss with 1 tablespoon of olive oil. Grease a 9-inch springform pan with olive oil.

2   In a large saucepan, heat 1 tablespoon olive oil and cook celery, carrots and onions in oil over medium heat until softened, about 5 minutes. Add pork and beef and sauté until browned and cooked through. Add the wine and let simmer for a few minutes. In bowl, crush the tomatoes using your hands, then add into the pan. Simmer for 5 to 10 minutes, using a wooden spoon to help break down the tomatoes further. Reduce heat to low and add the milk. Simmer for another 5 minutes. Season with salt and pepper to taste.

3   Mix the sauce into the bowl with cooked spaghetti and mix the egg thoroughly. Dump mixture into greased pan. Top with Parmesan. Bake at 375°F for 25 minutes or until the cheese is golden brown. Cut into slices and serve.

LAYERED LASAGNA

If you were a '90s baby like me, you may have grown up eating Stouffer's Lasagna. Those frozen lasagnas were like heaven with their soft pasta noodle sheets pillowed between warm ricotta cheese. This recipe calls for the sheets of creamy cheese and a broiled top, as well as béchamel sauce, ricotta pesto and kale filling with sausage. It is truly perfection.

SERVES 12

RICOTTA PESTO LAYER

15 ounces whole-milk ricotta cheese

¼ cup shredded Parmesan cheese

¾ cup (6.5 ounces) pesto

1 egg

¼ teaspoon salt

¼ teaspoon pepper

1   For Ricotta Pesto layer, mix all ingredients together in a medium bowl.

SAUSAGE KALE LAYER

1 tablespoon vegetable oil

1 pound mild Italian sausage

3 cloves garlic, minced

Pinch of crushed red pepper

4 cups kale, roughly chopped

1 15-ounce can tomato sauce

2 tablespoons sugar

Salt and black pepper, to taste

2   For Sausage Kale layer, heat oil in a large sauté pan and cook sausage until crumbled and brown. Add garlic and red pepper flakes and sauté until fragrant, about 30 seconds. Add the kale and cook until it is slightly wilted. Add tomato sauce and sugar and simmer the mixture for 5 minutes. Season with salt and black pepper to taste.

2 cups whole milk

¼ cup (4 tablespoons) unsalted butter

¼ cup flour

½ teaspoon salt

Pinch of black pepper

Pinch of nutmeg

3   For béchamel layer, heat milk in a microwave-safe measuring cup for 1 to 2 minutes until very warm. In a small saucepan, make a roux by melting butter on medium-low heat. When butter is melted, add flour and whisk until all the flour is incorporated and the mixture is a smooth paste. Slowly pour the heated milk into the paste mixture, whisking continuously until milk is fully mixed into paste and mixture is smooth. Simmer for 1 minute, until mixture is thick and coats the back of a spoon. Stir in salt, black pepper and nutmeg.

**14 ounces (about 15) lasagna sheets,
    cooked al dente and coated in olive oil**

½ cup Parmesan cheese, grated

4   To assemble lasagna, grease a 9-by-13-inch casserole dish with olive oil. Preheat oven to 350°F. Add half the Ricotta Pesto layer to the bottom of the casserole dish. Top with 3 sheets of lasagna noodles, spacing them out evenly to cover the whole dish. Add half the Sausage Kale layer and top with 3 more pasta sheets. Add half of the béchamel sauce, then another 3 pasta sheets. Repeat the process, using the rest of the layers, ending with béchamel on the top. Spread the béchamel evenly and smoothly over the top and sprinkle with ½ cup Parmesan cheese. Bake lasagna for 45 to 55 minutes, until heated through and golden-brown on top. Let rest for 15 minutes before serving.

Chapter Four

HOLIDAY TRADITIONS

Clam Chowder

Miso Maple Carrots

Figgy Ham

Scratch Gravy

Chorizo Cornbread Stuffing

Potato Chip–Crusted Creamed Corn

I've always believed that life is one big celebration asking us to join. I was usually the one in my family handing out kazoos hoping everyone would catch the party spirit. I have always wanted to celebrate every part of life, to count on and anticipate what each new season held. My family didn't observe American holidays with much gusto; we celebrated Christmas and gathered for Thanksgiving but we did it differently every year.

The only holiday my family celebrated was Chinese New Year. Our tradition was to gather for a large meal at a restaurant, reciting blessings to elders and receiving red envelopes of money. One Easter I saved my allowance money to buy plastic eggs filled with candy. I asked my mom to hide them around the house so my brother and I could have our own egg hunt.

But when my peers would return from their holidays and regale us with details about their holidays, I couldn't relate. I felt that I was missing out on a huge part of what the buzz was about. I felt disjointed to be living in a culture I didn't get to fully participate in.

My aunt (Ada Chan) once hosted a Thanksgiving dinner with roast duck and a store-bought pie. The red candles on the table surely made this the bona fide holiday that everyone had raved about. I was elated. For her, it was an afterthought; for me, it was something that would connect me with my American peers.

When I was 15, I was having a typical dim sum lunch with my mom's side of the family on Thanksgiving. After my meal, I walked to the grocery store across the street just to watch the lines of last-minute shoppers. Their urgency to be home with their groceries stressed the importance of the season. I felt an overwhelming need to be part of this collective occasion. I grabbed a cart, determined to attempt to make our first Thanksgiving dinner. My mom always supported my creative initiatives, so she happily paid for the groceries.

I only had clues about what to make by passing through the holiday aisles, in addition to the knowledge from what I had watched on cooking shows. I plopped a crouton stuffing mix, cans of cranberry sauce and gravy, and a frozen turkey into my cart. Later I learned about the minor details such as: the turkey needed to be defrosted overnight and the little bag of gizzards was meant to be put into the stuffing.

Around 6 p.m., I gathered my parents and brother at the table. The golden-brown turkey flowed with pink juices once I sliced into it. I didn't know what that meant until my mom hinted that it was still raw. Instead of placing it back into the oven, we ate around the center, eating only the drumsticks and wings, and tossing the rest. They ate only the dark meat drenched in gravy, and I realized my Cantonese family doesn't like dry food: Every savory dish must be wet or drowned in sauce.

Despite the turkey debacle, I found that day to be a success. I knew the food was bland and tasted like a commercial dinner, but it was on the table, and we were sitting around it, just like so many other families were that night.

Our Thanksgiving dinners have improved each year since then. My grandma's favorite is the clam chowder and ham, but she still brings foam to-go boxes filled with roast duck, soy sauce chicken, fried pork belly and barbecue pork. I just make the sides to accompany it. Yes, the plastic sauce cups mess up my Martha Stewart table-scape, but I've come to appreciate the "East meets West" approach to our Thanksgiving dinner.

CLAM CHOWDER

When I introduced Thanksgiving dinner to my family, it was not an instant crowd-pleaser. But once I added clam chowder to the menu, everyone suddenly became a fan. I make a pot of this every year—each time larger than the last—and it is always finished by the end of the evening.

SERVES 8

4 strips bacon, diced

2 carrots, diced

2 celery stalks, diced

2 red potatoes, diced

½ white onion, diced

1 (8-ounce) can clam juice

¾ cup (1½ sticks) unsalted butter

¾ cup flour

1 quart half-and-half

2 teaspoons Worcestershire sauce

1 cup canned clams, chopped

1 teaspoon dried thyme

1½ teaspoons salt

½ teaspoon cracked black pepper

2 teaspoons chopped fresh parsley,
   for garnish

1   In a sauté pan, sauté bacon until fat is rendered but bacon is not crispy. Add carrots, celery, red potatoes and onion and cook until onion is translucent, about 5 minutes.

2   Add clam juice and bring to a simmer. Continue to simmer until potatoes are tender, about 10 minutes.

3   In a soup pot on medium-low heat, make a roux by melting butter and slowly whisking in flour until creamy. Slowly pour in half-and-half, whisking constantly. Add Worcestershire sauce. Add clam meat and vegetable mixture. Season with thyme, salt and pepper. Serve and garnish with parsley.

MISO MAPLE CARROTS

I can't get enough of these roasted carrots. A traditional dish with an Asian staple perfectly highlights my family's "East meets West" Thanksgiving dinner.

SERVES 8

2 pounds whole carrots

3 tablespoons olive oil

3 tablespoons miso paste

½ teaspoon apple cider vinegar

1 tablespoon maple syrup

¼ teaspoon salt

Sesame seeds, for garnish

1   Preheat oven to 425°F. Place carrots in a sided sheet pan.

2   In a small bowl, mix olive oil, miso paste, apple cider vinegar, maple syrup and salt until smooth. Pour mixture onto the whole carrots, coating evenly.

3   Roast for 20 to 25 minutes until tender, rotating carrots as they roast. Garnish with sesame seeds.

FIGGY HAM

Every year for Thanksgiving, I make a ham and a turkey. One year I didn't buy an extra jar of jelly for the ham but found a jar of forgotten fig jam in the fridge. It ended up being a yummy surprise and turned the ham a beautiful deep red.

SERVES 8

2-pound ham steak

SPICE MIXTURE

1 teaspoon pumpkin spice

¼ cup brown sugar

GLAZE

⅓ cup (4.5 ounces) fig jam

¾ cup (6 ounces) dark soda (cola, root beer; no diet drinks)

1   Pat ham dry. Mix pumpkin spice and brown sugar together in a small bowl. Massage onto ham and refrigerate overnight.

2   The next day, preheat oven to 350°F.

3   To make the glaze, mix together jam and soda in a small saucepan over medium heat. Bring to a simmer, and cook, stirring occasionally until it thickens, about 10 to 15 minutes.

4   Meanwhile, place the ham in a roasting pan and bake in the oven. After 15 minutes, spoon half the glaze over the ham steak. Bake ham for another 25 to 45 minutes, depending on the size of your ham steak. Occasionally baste the ham as it finishes cooking with the remaining glaze.

SCRATCH GRAVY

I also call this the "forgivable gravy" because it's different every year yet it always manages to taste delicious. The meat marinades are different each year—some saltier than others, so no two gravies will be exactly alike. The key is obtaining the perfect balance of salt and creaminess. I would recommend adjusting your gravy by taste and not by ingredients.

SERVES 8

1 tablespoon butter

1 tablespoon flour

1 cup meat drippings, fat skimmed off

2 tablespoons red or white wine, depending on if it's a dark or light-colored gravy

Salt and white pepper, to taste

Sprig of fresh thyme (optional)

2 tablespoons heavy cream (optional)

1   In a small saucepan, melt butter and slowly whisk in flour. When combined, add meat drippings and whisk until smooth.

2   At this point, add the wine and thyme leaves, and bring to a simmer. Let simmer for 5 minutes. Season to taste with salt and white pepper. For extra decadence, mix in the heavy cream at the end.

CHORIZO CORNBREAD STUFFING

This stuffing balances sweet and savory tones: sweetness from the cornbread and savory from the spicy chorizo. It makes a decadent side to your turkey and has become my holiday favorite.

SERVES 8

3 garlic cloves, minced

½ onion, diced

2 celery stalks, diced

2 carrots, diced

½ red bell pepper, diced

1 pound chorizo

1 (9-by-9-inch) tray stale cornbread, cut into ½ inch cubes

½ cup chicken broth

½ cup half-and-half

1   Preheat the oven to 350°F. Grease a casserole dish with butter.

2   In a large, deep-sided sauté pan, sauté garlic and veggies together until translucent, about 10 minutes.

3   Add chorizo and break up into crumbles as it browns. Continue cooking until chorizo is cooked through. Add cornbread, folding it into the mixture. Pour in chicken broth and half-and-half.

4   Place the stuffing into the buttered 9-by-13-inch casserole dish and bake for 30 to 35 minutes.

POTATO CHIP-CRUSTED CREAMED CORN

My family loves sweet yellow corn. I like to make this for Thanksgiving with leftover béchamel sauce. This can be prepared ahead of time, then sprinkled with potato chip crust when it's time to eat.

SERVES 8

BÉCHAMEL SAUCE

2 cups whole milk

¼ cup (4 tablespoons) unsalted butter

¼ cup flour

½ teaspoon salt

Pinch of black pepper

Pinch of nutmeg

POTATO CHIP CRUST

3 tablespoons butter

2 tablespoons olive oil

1 (7-ounce) bag potato chips, crumbled

½ cup Parmesan cheese, grated

¼ cup parsley, chopped

Crumbled bacon (optional)

5 cups frozen sweet corn

1   For the béchamel sauce, heat milk in a microwave-safe measuring cup for 1 to 2 minutes until very warm. In a small saucepan, make a roux by melting butter on medium-low heat. When butter is melted, add flour and whisk until all the flour is incorporated and the mixture is a smooth paste. Slowly pour the heated milk into the paste mixture, whisking continuously until milk is fully mixed into paste and mixture is smooth. Simmer for 1 minute, until mixture is thick and coats the back of a spoon. Keep warm over low heat.

2   In a medium skillet, heat butter and olive oil over medium heat. Add crumbled potato chips and toast until golden brown. Remove from heat and add Parmesan cheese and parsley.

3   Cook the corn in a microwave or on the stove-top according to package instructions, until heated through. Add corn to a casserole dish. Pour the hot béchamel sauce over the corn and mix together. Garnish with the toasted potato chips and crumbled bacon. Serve hot.

As a latchkey kid, I spent many afternoons at my friends' homes. My friends and their families embraced this awkward tween who had little idea about her identity or belonging.

My closest friend, Alexis, the most glamorous girl in junior high, took me under her wing by inviting me to her birthday party after I'd thrown spitballs at her in class. She was enigmatic— half Chinese, half African-American—with an exotic style: silk scarves from India, earrings from Morocco, leather boots from Italy. She was that girl who showed up to prom in a red and gold sari while every other girl wore a dress. I was interested in who she was, so I did what any normal preteen would do and hit her with a spitball. She somehow took this delinquency as an opportunity for friendship, and before long we were watching TV and eating dinner on her couch.

Her mother, Gwen, is one of the most glamorous women I have ever known. She is a headstrong, down-to-earth businesswoman, with Creole roots and exotic tastes. Her home and wardrobe were filled with keepsakes from places to which she had traveled. She drove us around in her black Cadillac Escalade, listened to R&B and rap music and told us about doing good in the world. Her house smelled like cinnamon candles, and she made cider in a pot that could feed the masses. Her home was warm and inviting, something you knew you wanted to be a part of the moment you walked in.

Whenever I visited them, it was assumed I'd be joining them for dinner, which we usually ate in their living room while watching movies. Although both she and her husband worked, and she had a few businesses of her own, they still cooked homemade meals from an array of different ethnic cuisines. Their fridge was always stocked with fresh food, the freezer filled with a variety of ice cream flavors, and there were two large cabinets filled entirely with herbs and spices. Having whipped pretend ingredients in bowls for years dreaming about a perfect recipe, I saw Gwen's lifestyle as one great Pandora's box of possibilities. A single kitchen cabinet had more options than my entire kitchen, and she let me use all the gadgets and ingredients I needed to experiment with any recipe I desired.

Before I met Alexis, I had only eaten Chinese and American food. Gwen took us out to dinner at exotic restaurants where she introduced me to Peruvian Lomo Saltado with Inca Kola, Brazilian grilled meats, Afghan and Mediterranean food with spiced skewered chicken. She always shared in detail about the culture of the cuisine we were eating. Although I wasn't always enticed by the different foods and the bold flavors, her sense of connecting cultures through food was more than intriguing.

Alexis and I spent hours in the kitchen assisting with dinner time. While chopping vegetables and drying dishes, we talked about our families and our own cultural identities. During those tender years, I was confused about my place in the world and how to act in it. I was an itty-bitty preteen with a foul mouth and no manners. Gwen had a gift. She knew how to love without shaming any shortcomings. She fostered the best in me while allowing the space for where I was at the time.

Gwen's "hostess with the mostest" lifestyle was something she passed on to me, or maybe something I'd been eager to find all along. I had felt sheltered as a youngster, but from what I wasn't sure. Gwen threw open the doors of everything I could be, everything there was to experience—from a deep-fried seasoned turkey at Thanksgiving time to the cultures of countries I'd never heard of.

She later told me, after I had decided to go to culinary school, that she didn't know why I hadn't done that all along, since she had rarely seen me out of her kitchen. I wonder how many times she had seen me all those years and known I was growing up in her kitchen.

One of the kindest women I knew was my friend Sam's mother, who I called Tita (Aunt) Beth. She all but adopted me during middle school. She was a woman who took in strays—particularly ones in hand-me-downs. She included me in shopping trips and dinners and made me feel like part of her family. Sam and I watched the Food Network and bad reality TV all day on her couch in between soccer practices. When it got late, Tita Beth would offer to have me sleep over, then take me to school the next day. She gave me a place at her table in every way possible.

Her benevolence meant even more to me when I later learned that, in addition to being a mother of four, she had a full-time job. She was the type of woman who would drop her busy schedule to attend to something her child needed. On top of that, she also had a side hustle selling chocolate bars with specialized photos on the labels. She employed Sam and me to glue on the paper labels and paid us for the dozen or so we wrapped as if we had completed the full order. Whenever we went shopping, she bought something for me as well as Sam.

One of my fondest memories of Tita Beth was a night several of us girls were sleeping over with Sam, making entirely too much noise. At 2:00 a.m., a soft knock rapped at the door, and in came Tita Beth with a tray of gourmet cookies and a huge smile on her face. "Cookies?" she said.

She fed everyone. She introduced me to Filipino food, which she cooked for the Bible study gatherings she hosted. I looked forward to those gatherings since I knew she would make sweet red Filipino spaghetti. I wasn't a believer in the dish when I first watched her prepare it—chopping up hot dog links and pouring sugar into the sauce—but I turned out to be an easy convert. I endured the regular Bible studies in exchange for time with her and Sam, and Filipino spaghetti, and maybe that's what they were really about.

Parenthood must be the curation of selflessness with the knowledge that you can never be paid back. Gwen and Tita Beth had it in spades, for all the kids who walked through their doors.

BROWN SUGAR DIP

I tried this dip for the first time at Alexis' house. She makes this simple, three-ingredient dip for family gatherings. The combination of sour cream and brown sugar makes it captivating at first bite for its unique contrast of sweet and tang.

SERVES 6

1 cup sour cream

3 tablespoons brown sugar

1 teaspoon vanilla extract

5 cups fresh fruit (blackberries, raspberries, blueberries, mango, peaches)

Combine all ingredients, except the fruit, in a small bowl. Refrigerate for 30 minutes. Serve with fruit.

SUN-DRIED TOMATO PESTO DIP

This is still the go-to dip for Alexis and me. The Parmesan cheese, walnuts and sun-dried tomatoes give a host of different flavors: savory, nutty and sweet all in one bite. Best served on a baguette. Careful, this is addicting!

SERVES 6

1 cup sun-dried tomatoes

3 tablespoons oil from
  sun-dried tomatoes

2 cloves garlic

½ cup fresh basil leaves

¾ cup Parmesan cheese, grated

⅓ cup walnuts

1 tablespoon balsamic vinegar

½ cup olive oil

½ teaspoon salt

¼ teaspoon black pepper

1   Combine the sun-dried tomatoes, oil, garlic, basil, Parmesan cheese, walnuts, balsamic vinegar and sugar into a food processor and pulse.

2   Gradually add olive oil as it blends. Mixture should be slightly chunky.

3   Serve in a dipping bowl alongside a crusty baguette.

FILIPINO SPAGHETTI

Tita Beth hosted dinners for her friends from time to time. She would make a huge pot of this irresistible sweet sauce and a pot of spaghetti. This was the type of meal that you would walk up to the stove and serve yourself. I'll be the first to admit that I once was skeptical about a sweet sauce with sausage, but now I am a believer. It all just works!

SERVES 6

3 tablespoons vegetable oil

3 tablespoons garlic, minced

1 yellow or white onion, minced

1 bell pepper, seeded and chopped finely

1 pound ground pork

8 hot dogs, sliced diagonally into ½-inch pieces

1 15-ounce can (1½ cups) tomato sauce

2 tablespoons to ¼ cup sugar, or to taste

¼ cup evaporated milk

1 pound cooked spaghetti noodles, for serving

½ cup shredded cheddar cheese or Parmesan cheese, for serving

1   In a medium pan, sauté garlic, onions and bell peppers in vegetable oil over medium heat. Cook until translucent about 3 to 4 minutes.

2   Add the ground pork and hot dog links, and sauté until lightly browned. Add tomato sauce, sugar and evaporated milk. Bring to a boil. Simmer for 30 minutes.

3   Season to taste with salt and pepper. Serve over a bed of spaghetti and top with shredded cheddar cheese or Parmesan cheese.

CHICKEN & VEGGIE KEBABS

My friend Alexis has a fascination with Mediterranean and Middle Eastern cultures, particularly the cuisine. She was the first one to show me all the different spices, plus a new way to cook chicken. The yogurt in this marinade is what hydrates the chicken and makes it extra juicy.

MAKES 6 KEBABS

1 pound boneless, skinless chicken thighs, cut into 1-inch pieces

1 teaspoon salt

1 teaspoon black pepper

1 teaspoon lemon zest

3 tablespoons lemon juice

3 tablespoons olive oil

3 garlic cloves, minced

1 teaspoon turmeric

Pinch of red pepper flakes

¼ cup Greek yogurt

½ cup colorful veggies such as onions and bell peppers

1   If using wooden skewers, soak them in water overnight.

2   The next day, preheat the oven to 350°F. Place chicken in a large bowl and season with salt and black pepper. Mix in lemon zest, lemon juice, olive oil, garlic, turmeric, red pepper flakes and yogurt together with chicken. Let the chicken marinate for 1 hour.

3   Skewer chicken and vegetables onto wooden skewers. Place kebabs on a baking sheet, and bake for 7 minutes, then flip skewers and bake for another 7 minutes. Change oven to broil setting and broil for 1 minute. Serve over basmati rice or with naan bread.

LOMO SALTADO

Gwen, my mentor as a teen, introduced me to Peruvian cuisine when she took me to a family-owned restaurant. I was fascinated by the combination of flavors and the Inca Kola we drank with the meal. This stir-fry recipe includes steak, french fries and tomatoes, and is served over rice. The cool green sauce on the side cuts the heaviness of the meal.

CILANTRO SAUCE

1 medium jalapeño pepper, roughly chopped

⅓ cup mayonnaise

3 tablespoons lime juice

¼ cup cilantro

½ cup iceberg lettuce

1 teaspoon salt

Cracked black pepper

2 tablespoons vegetable oil

2 garlic cloves, minced

1 teaspoon minced jalapeño peppers

½ cup sliced red onion

1 pound boneless rib eye, thinly sliced

1 tablespoon cumin

2 tablespoons soy sauce

2 tablespoons vinegar

2 cups cooked french fries

2 medium tomatoes (cut into 6 wedges)

Salt and black pepper, to taste

Cilantro, for garnish

2 cups cooked white rice, for serving

SERVES 2

1   For the cilantro sauce, blend all the ingredients in a blender until smooth. Season with salt and black pepper and refrigerate until ready to use.

2   In a large sauté pan, heat oil and sauté garlic, jalapeños and onions over medium-high heat. Add rib eye and cumin.

3   When the meat is charred, add soy sauce and vinegar. Add french fries and tomatoes, tossing gently. Add salt and pepper to taste.

4   To serve, garnish with cilantro leaves and a drizzle of the green cilantro sauce. Serve with white rice.

INDIAN BUTTER CHICKEN

In high school, Alexis befriended a girl named Candice, who was Indian and just so happened to live a block away from Alexis' home. Alexis was frequently at her house and instantly became a fan of Indian food. When Candice moved away to college, Alexis' cravings still drove her (and me with her) to the few Indian eateries in our area. My first bite of Indian food was life-changing and once again gave me a love for new spices.

SERVES 4

2 teaspoons garam masala

2 teaspoons turmeric

1 teaspoon chili powder

1 teaspoon cumin

1 pound boneless, skinless chicken thighs
   or breasts, cut into ¾-inch pieces

1 teaspoon salt

¼ teaspoon black pepper

¼ cup plain whole-milk yogurt

½ cup (1 stick) unsalted butter

1 white onion, sliced

3 garlic cloves, minced

1 tablespoon ginger, minced

1 jalapeño pepper, minced

1 (15-ounce) can tomato sauce

1 cup half-and-half (room temperature)

Cilantro, for garnish

Basmati rice or naan

1   In a small bowl, combine garam masala, turmeric, chili powder and cumin.

2   In a medium bowl, add chicken cubes. Season with salt and black pepper. Add ¼ cup yogurt and 1 tablespoon of powdered spice blend. Let the chicken marinate for 30 minutes.

3   In a large sauté pan, melt the butter over medium heat and then sauté the onions until they begin to soften, about 5 minutes. Add garlic, ginger and jalapeño along with the rest of the powdered spice blend. Cook until the onions have become translucent. Add tomato sauce.

4   In a small bowl, mix a few tablespoons of tomato sauce into half-and-half. Add the half-and-half mixture to the rest of the tomato sauce in the pan. Bring to a simmer and add the marinated chicken to the tomato sauce. Let simmer until chicken is fully cooked, about 15 to 20 minutes. Serve with naan or basmati rice.

Chapter Six

MAKING PEACE
WITH FOOD

Béchamel Sauce

Foolproof Vinaigrette

Greek Panzanella

Harissa Spatchcock Chicken

Papillote Fish

Drunken Steak

For most of my teenage years, I was afraid to be by myself. Underneath a facade of confidence, a fear of some void lingered. Without validation or distraction from others, I didn't feel worthwhile, much less content. I was torn between appreciating myself for who I had become and still not fully committing to loving myself. I loved my creativity and whimsical personality, but I also hated my nagging insecurity.

I was coming of age at a time when Christina Aguilera's stick-thin body was the enviable figure for young women. Even though I loved playing soccer and it helped me feel like I was fitting in, it gave me muscular thighs that some relatives made me feel self-conscious about. I was told I was losing my femininity and would have fewer prospects for marriage because my thighs had become too muscular. A close female relative even took a photo of me in a swimsuit to give me perspective on my looming demise due to—tragically!—those blasted soccer thighs.

While my relative surely meant well, I became fixated on wanting a completely different body frame. Dressing rooms were nightmares, and school became a breeding ground for feelings of insecurity and inferiority. I had the habit of scanning the crowds for any girl whose figure I wished were mine, and mentally photoshopping my head on her body.

In Chinese culture, it's not uncommon to criticize other people's appearances. I didn't know any other curvy Asian girls and it made me feel like I was sort of fat. I started to become obsessively afraid of being overweight. Being a foodie yet anxious about every bite I ate only created a cycle of militant rules followed by shame for failing. As I entered culinary school, my eating habits became worse. After cooking our meal assignments, the chef would taste and critique our food. We then had five minutes to eat before cleaning up.

My culinary peers and I learned to consume our meals quickly before tossing the rest in the trash. Eating became more about finishing than savoring. When each meal regularly called for several sticks of butter, I mentally blanked out while eating to avoid thinking about the number of calories I was consuming. The mere feeling of being full filled me with remorse.

For an entire year I raced to the gym near school, sometimes twice a day. I would eat a healthy meal for breakfast and lunch, then binge late at night. I would wake up the next morning ridden with guilt and try to "fix it" by beginning the same cycle again. Eventually, I became so weary of the overwhelming guilt every night, I started getting more creative with the healthy meals I cooked—adding flavors and textures into recipes in unexpected ways.

As ironic as it sounds, it was then that I took refuge in cooking almost as a meditative practice. When insecurity and my fear of not having enough created a state of almost constant anxiety, it was the slow and ordered practice of cooking a meal that was my saving grace.

It was in the kitchen that I learned to enjoy my own company, often while cooking late into the night. The kitchen was my haven of solitude where I learned to process emotions I hadn't been able to—or hadn't been aware of—elsewhere. It was also a place meant for experimenting, and I could do it to my heart's content without the repercussions so common in youth. For the first time, I was experimenting for the right reasons.

The process of cooking, particularly the time I spent alone, cultivated an equanimity I had not known before. I appreciated myself. For the first time, I wasn't running away from myself; I was engaging in the present moment. I was at home in the kitchen.

BÉCHAMEL SAUCE

I call this the granddaddy of all sauces and the foundation of many great dishes. Of all the classical French sauces I learned in culinary school, this is the one I remember. Master this sauce and you can whip up homemade mac and cheese, a cheese fondue or Alfredo at a moment's notice.

MAKES ABOUT 2 CUPS

2 cups whole milk

¼ cup unsalted butter

¼ cup flour

½ teaspoon salt

Pinch of black pepper

Pinch of nutmeg

1   Heat milk in a microwave-safe measuring cup for 2 to 3 minutes until very warm.

2   In a small saucepan, make a roux by melting butter on medium-low heat. When butter is melted, add flour and whisk until all the flour is incorporated and the mixture is a smooth paste.

3   Slowly pour the heated milk into the paste mixture, whisking continuously until milk is fully mixed into paste and mixture is smooth. Simmer for 1 minute, until mixture is thick and coats the back of a spoon. Stir in salt, black pepper and nutmeg.

VARIATIONS

MACARONI AND CHEESE
Add 1 cup of your favorite grated cheese (or a combination of cheeses!), such as cheddar, Gouda or fontina.

ALFREDO
Pour sauce on top of your favorite cooked pasta noodles.

CHEESE FONDUE
Mix in grated Gruyère and Swiss cheese and transfer into a fondue pot set over warm heat. Add a dash of dry mustard and a splash of white wine. Serve with cubes of French bread, veggies and cooked meats.

FOOLPROOF VINAIGRETTE

The cardinal rule taught in culinary school is to season or dress everything. This is an easy vinaigrette that can be made fresh in a minute. A lot of these ingredients are most likely in your kitchen already: any oils and vinegars can be used to make this dressing.

MAKES 1 CUP

¼ cup vinegar of choice, such as apple cider or balsamic

¾ cup oil of choice, such as olive or sunflower

1 tablespoon Dijon mustard

1 tablespoon honey

Salt and black pepper, to taste

Place all ingredients in a Mason jar and shake it up!

GREEK PANZANELLA

This was my favorite dish I learned in culinary school. Cold, crunchy and refreshing veggies alongside soaked croutons. Thanks to this panzanella, it's okay to be the "salad girl."

SERVES 6

3 tablespoons unsalted butter

3 cups hard crusty bread, cut into 1-inch cubes

1½ cups cherry tomatoes, cut in half

¼ cup red onions, thinly sliced

1 cup yellow bell pepper, cubed

½ cup pitted kalamata olives

1 cucumber, cut into 1-inch pieces

½ cup feta cheese, cut into ½ cubes

¼ cup Foolproof Vinaigrette (see p. 102)

¼ cup pomegranate seeds, for garnish (optional)

Salt and black pepper, to taste

1   In a large sauté pan, melt the butter over medium-low heat. Add the bread cubes and coat in butter. Toast until all the surfaces have a slightly golden color, tossing the bread cubes in the pan every so often.

2   In a large bowl, mix veggies and feta together, and toss with the Foolproof Vinaigrette. Season to taste with salt and black pepper. Gently stir in the bread cubes and serve immediately.

HARISSA SPATCHCOCK CHICKEN

This is a great recipe for the impatient cook, such as myself. With the spatchcock technique, when you remove the chicken's backbone, you can have a roasted dinner in less than an hour. Adding the harissa into the butter mixture gives the chicken a rich flavor, plus a shiny red crust.

SERVES 4

¼ cup unsalted butter (room temperature)

2 tablespoons harissa paste

1 whole chicken (3-4 pounds)

1 bulb of garlic, cut in half

2 lemons, cut in half

Kosher salt, to taste

Cracked black pepper, to taste

1   Preheat oven to 425°F.

2   In a bowl, mix butter and harissa together.

3   Using kitchen shears, cut through chicken's backbone and remove the spine. Keep the spine for another use, such as making stock. Turn chicken breast upside down and flatten the chicken. Rub the harissa butter all over the chicken, even getting the harissa butter under the skin. Season the chicken generously with salt and black pepper.

4   Place chicken in a roasting pan or sided baking sheet. Add lemon halves and garlic halves. Roast 45 to 50 minutes. Baste the chicken halfway through the roasting process with lemon and garlic juices in the pan. Roast until the thermometer inserted into the thigh reads 165°F and juices run clear.

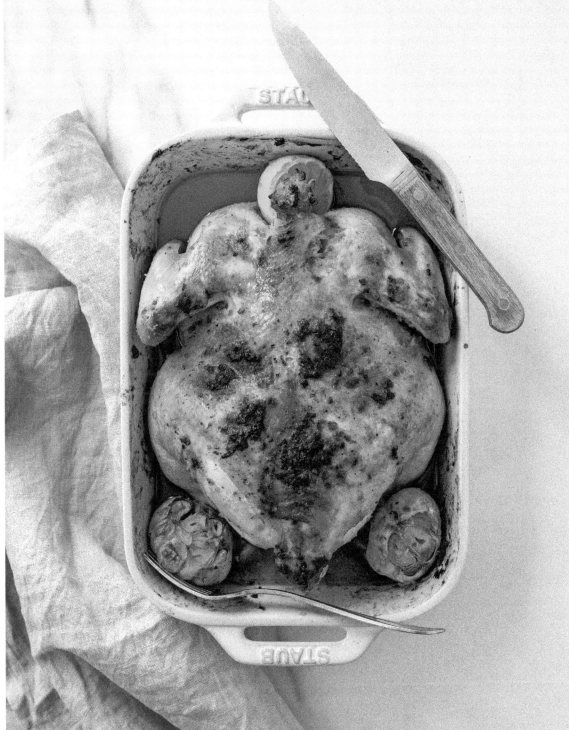

PAPILLOTE FISH

I've always loved unwrapping gifts. Even if it wasn't something I wanted, the euphoric feeling of unwrapping a surprise was just as exciting as the gift itself. When I learned how to make a papillote fish in culinary school, I knew that I wanted to surprise others and give them the same kind of feeling. I've made this dish with many different types of fish and vegetables, so add your own flair!

SERVES 2

1 cup vegetables, sliced into bite-size pieces (choice of zucchini, cherry tomatoes, asparagus, thinly slice parboiled potatoes)

2 tablespoons olive oil, divided

Salt and black pepper, to taste

2 (5-6 ounce) skin-on salmon fillets

2 thyme sprigs

4 lemons slices

1. Preheat oven to 450°F.

2. In a bowl, toss vegetables in 1 tablespoon olive oil, salt and pepper.

3. Cut two heart-shaped pieces of parchment paper or foil and fold in half, dividing the heart in two.

4. Lay the papers flat, and on one side of the heart, place the vegetables, dividing between the two pieces of parchment paper. Top vegetables with the salmon fillets. Season the salmon with salt and pepper, drizzle with remaining olive oil, and garnish with fresh herbs and lemon slices.

5. Crimp edges to form a sealed packet. Make a small slit at the top of the packet. Bake for 12 to 15 minutes.

DRUNKEN STEAK

On my 15th birthday, I wanted to impress my high-school boyfriend and two girlfriends with my cooking skills. I sautéed steak in wine as I had seen chefs on TV do—never mind that I added half a bottle. Next thing you know, we were all on a bench at the mall buzzed. Since then, I've learned that I was trying to re-create a wine reduction sauce. This is a tribute to my drunken steak many years ago.

SERVES 2

1 pound bone-in rib eye steak

Salt and black pepper

3 tablespoons unsalted butter

3 whole garlic cloves, smashed

2 thyme sprigs

¼ cup red wine

1   Let steak sit at room temperature for 30 minutes. Season steak generously with salt and black pepper.

2   Melt butter in a pan over medium heat. Turn the heat to medium-high, and add steak, garlic cloves and herbs. Sear for 5 minutes, then flip steak over and baste with butter. Cook for another 5 minutes until medium-rare. Transfer steak to cutting board and let it rest for at least 10 minutes.

3   In the same pan, add red wine and let it reduce to half its volume. Pour over steak and serve.

Chapter Seven

KITCHEN DETOUR

Split Pea Soup

Hoisin Sticky Ribs

Tuna Chip Casserole

Chipotle Tofu Steak

Cranberry Meat Loaf

Garlic Roast Pork

I have never been a natural academic. Personal projects have always been far more engrossing to me than grinding away at books. I dreamed my way through class, submitted assignments at my leisure and couldn't sit still long enough to hear an entire lecture. In fact, as early as grade school, it seemed to me that school existed more as an entity to stunt my growth—merely time away from my own projects I was eager to get back to.

I was nearly held back in the fifth grade due to my poor performance and class clownery. After that year—nearly being held back and having poor relationships with teachers—school became a place entirely for social experiments, not for learning. Getting away with skipping classes was one popular experiment.

Nobody knew why I was acting out. Aside from feeling suffocated by a classroom style of learning, I felt out of place as an individual. I was uncomfortable for not being "American" enough, for not having the latest or shiniest things, even being in my own skin. I pretended that I fit in, but knew that I was fundamentally different—in looks, status and performance.

In high school, when most of my classmates were preparing their college applications, my focus was on finding ways to get into the local nightclubs. After graduation, I ended up in a community college and quit after one semester. Having been convinced by that point that I was incapable of succeeding in a school setting, I was stumped. A conventional path wasn't appealing, and I was running out of ideas.

I had always cooked for all my friends, whether it was for a party at my place or just before we went out. Loving food as much as I did, it was oddly never something I gave a second thought to pursuing more than casually. However, at the suggestion of friends who proved to know me better than I knew myself, I enrolled in a local culinary school.

School became a completely new experience. While very structured, the style of learning in culinary school is completely hands-on. Even if a task was as menial as washing the dishes, it was applicable to real life; I could engage with it, watch it change in my hands, I could get messy. Walking through a process and seeing the end of it on my plate was the finality I needed that I never found in a textbook. Theories and hypotheses were painfully irrelevant. In the kitchen, I was creating.

I went from trying to get a passing grade with the least amount of work to being an overachiever. Many of the things I made in class I would later remake at home, spinning a classic dish with my own flair or trying to find shortcuts. I learned the rules with as much precision as I could so I could break them later. At first, I was reprimanded for going off track, but eventually the chefs started complimenting the subtle differences in ingredients or way of plating the dish. When I wasn't at school cooking or learning, I was at home practicing new techniques and recipes. I spent much of my time watching cooking shows, trying new restaurants and finding hands-on opportunities to broaden my scope of the culinary world.

Midway through culinary school, I took a position creating recipes at the employee cafeteria for the San Jose Mercury News media company. This was the playground I had always craved. Creativity was at the heart of the role, but structure was still there making sure I didn't get blown to the wind. Creativity and structure found an equilibrium, and I finally saw how each complements the other. While too little freedom can be repulsive, too much freedom may be its sinister cousin. We can get scattered in our quest for freedom, our creativity wasted. The structure that helped me create opened my eyes to how I learn and what I could accomplish when given the right setting.

I also realized what I ultimately wanted to do with food was share it. The food we remember and love is what we have shared with those around us. Cooking is the first step, but only the first. Around the table is where it matters.

SPLIT PEA SOUP

This recipe takes about 5 minutes to assemble and another hour for the peas to become smooth. With chopped celery and carrots, plus onions and ham for flavor, this is a wholesome meal that comes out delicious every time.

SERVES 6

2 carrots, minced

2 celery stalks, minced

½ onion, minced

2 tablespoons vegetable oil

½ pound ham, diced

1 ham hock

1 pound dried split peas

2 sprigs fresh thyme

1 bay leaf

1 teaspoon balsamic vinegar

10 cups low-sodium chicken stock

¼ teaspoon salt and pepper, or to taste

Microgreens, for garnish (optional)

1   In a soup pot, sauté the vegetables in oil on medium heat until translucent, about 5 minutes. Add the ham and ham hock, and brown it on its sides. Add the split peas. Add thyme, bay leaf, balsamic vinegar and chicken stock. Bring to a simmer until split peas have sprouted.

2   After about 1 hour, when the split peas are tender, adjust the consistency of the soup with water or broth if the soup becomes too thick or dry.

3   Scrape all the meat from ham hock and put back into the soup. Discard the ham bone. Season to taste with salt and pepper.

HOISIN STICKY RIBS

One of the first things I made when I started to experiment in the kitchen was baby back ribs. A good seasoning and a decent sauce are really all you need. The hoisin sauce on these ribs is my Asian twist. The meat comes off the bone tender and sticky. Bon appétit!

SERVES 4

2 slabs baby back ribs

1 teaspoon salt

½ teaspoon white pepper

1 teaspoon chili oil

⅓ cup hoisin sauce

1 teaspoon ginger, grated

2 teaspoons rice wine vinegar

1 tablespoon ketchup

½ teaspoon Chinese five-spice powder

Sesame seeds, for garnish

1   Preheat oven to 275°F. Season ribs all over with salt and white pepper.

2   In a medium bowl, add chili oil, hoisin sauce, ginger, rice wine vinegar, ketchup and five-spice powder. Using a pastry brush, coat seasoned ribs with sauce. Set aside any leftover sauce. Wrap each rib tightly in foil and place on a baking sheet. Bake for 3½ to 4 hours, until a fork can easily slide into the meat between the bones.

3   Carefully unwrap the ribs and baste with reserved sauce. For extra caramelization, place ribs without the foil back on the baking sheet and run them under the broiler for a few minutes. Slice ribs and garnish with sesame seeds.

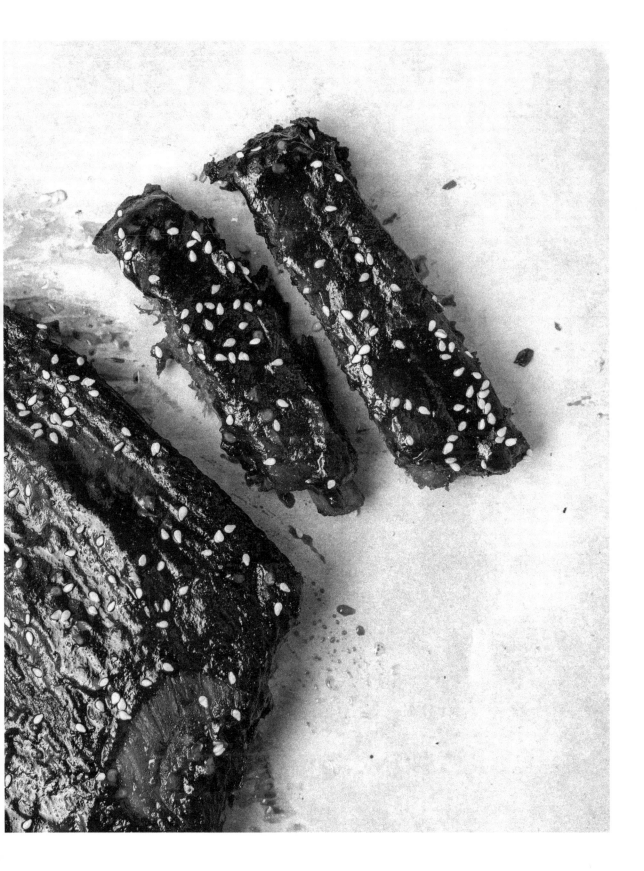

TUNA CHIP CASSEROLE

If you're looking to make a dish with ingredients you already have stocked, this casserole is a wonderful option. Just canned tuna, frozen peas, frozen carrots and pasta, then topped off with Parmesan potato-chip crust. It was the first lunch item I ever made at the cafeteria, and one that's not hard to feel sentimental over.

SERVES 6

12 ounces pasta noodles (of your choice)

¼ cup unsalted butter

¼ cup flour

2 cups half-and-half

1 teaspoon Dijon mustard

1 teaspoon Worcestershire sauce

1 cup frozen mixed vegetables (peas, carrots and corn)

2 (5-ounce) cans tuna

1 tablespoon olive oil

¼ cup pasta starch water

POTATO CHIP TOPPING

3 tablespoons butter

1½ cup potato chips, crushed

⅓ cup Parmesan cheese, grated

1 tablespoon fresh parsley, chopped

1   In a large pot, boil about 4 quarts water with a generous amount of salt. Add noodles to boiling water. For al dente noodles, follow package instructions but subtract one minute. Once pasta is cooked, reserve ¼ cup pasta water and drain the rest. Toss the pasta in olive oil to keep the pasta from sticking.

2   In another saucepan, melt butter and slowly whisk in flour. Once incorporated, add half-and-half, Dijon mustard and Worcestershire sauce. Add reserved pasta water to thin out the sauce, as needed. Remove from heat.

3   In the bowl with the pasta, add peas, carrots and tuna. Add the cream sauce and stir. Pour into casserole dish.

4   For the Potato Chip Topping, melt butter on medium-low heat in a saucepan. Add crushed potato chips into pan. Sauté chips until golden, and then add cheese and fresh parsley.

5   Sprinkle potato chip mixture on top of tuna pasta mixture. Set it to broil in your oven for about 1 minute, until golden brown on top and heated through.

CHIPOTLE TOFU STEAK

A firm slab of tofu can be a lighter substitute steak. The tofu retains the dark color from the marinade and has a surprisingly rich taste.

SERVES 4

2 tablespoons canned chipotle peppers in adobo sauce, finely chopped

1 tablespoon yellow mustard

2 tablespoons honey

2 tablespoons sesame oil

1 teaspoon soy sauce

1 (16-ounce) box firm tofu (cut into 8 pieces, lengthwise)

3 tablespoons vegetable oil

Chopped scallions or cilantro, for garnish

1   In a blender, blend chipotle peppers, 1 tablespoon adobo sauce reserved from the can, mustard, honey, sesame oil and soy sauce. Lay tofu into a small container. Pour mixture on top and let sit for 1 to 2 hours or overnight to marinate.

2   In a large pan on medium-low heat, add vegetable oil. Take tofu out of marinade, and sear tofu on both sides, 2 to 3 minutes per side. Remove tofu from pan.

3   Pour remaining marinade into the pan and simmer for 1 to 2 minutes. Pour over tofu and serve. Garnish with scallions or cilantro.

MELTING POT

CRANBERRY MEAT LOAF

I created this recipe when I was cooking for the employee cafeteria and it became an instant hit. Employees began buying extra meals to take to their families for dinner, which started our meat loaf takeout program. This famous meat loaf has a few tricks. While most meat loaf recipes use ground breadcrumbs, this one calls for torn white bread soaked in milk and eggs, which produces a more tender meat. The veggies are lightly sautéed before adding into the meat mixture. The real secret to flavoring is the packets of dried onion soup mix.

SERVES 6

⅓ cup ketchup

⅓ cup canned cranberry sauce

⅓ cup barbecue sauce

2 cups torn white bread or bread rolls

¼ cup whole milk

1 egg

1 carrot, diced

1 celery stalk, diced

½ white onion, diced

1 pound ground beef

1 packet dried onion soup mix

1 tablespoon Worcestershire sauce

1 Preheat oven to 350°F. In a small bowl, mix ketchup, barbecue sauce and cranberry sauce. Set aside.

2 In a large bowl, mix torn bread, milk and egg together. Using your hands, massage the mixture until clumpy, but not smooth.

3 In a small saucepan, sauté carrots, celery and onion over medium heat until translucent, about 5 minutes. Take off the heat and let cool slightly.

4 In another large bowl, combine beef, soup packet, Worcestershire sauce and veggies. Add ½ cup meat loaf sauce into the meat mixture. Add the soaked bread into the meat and blend with your hands, until mixture is homogeneous.

5 Place the meat mixture in a loaf pan and bake for 1 hour, until the center of the meat loaf reads 165°F on a thermometer. Baste with the meat loaf sauce after 30 minutes and reserve some sauce for serving.

GARLIC ROAST PORK

This recipe is budget-friendly and great when you're feeding a huge group. It can be as easy or complex as you want to make it. To keep it simple, you can buy an all-in-one dry seasoning and your favorite liquid sauce. This pork can be used for sandwiches, quesadillas, pizzas, salads and even for taco night.

SERVES 8

1 6-7-pound boneless pork shoulder (shoulder with fat)

2 tablespoons salt

1 tablespoon black pepper

1 onion, roughly chopped

1 head of garlic, individual cloves peeled

½ cup dry white wine

2 cups liquid of choice, such as broth or apple juice (for pulled pork variation)

1 Using a sharp knife, make hashtag slits in the fatty side of the pork shoulder. Insert knife all over the pork with different depth cuts and add garlic slivers into incisions. Rub the pork shoulder with the salt and black pepper.

2 Put the pork in a pan or a large ziplock bag. Add onions and the wine. Cover the pork and let it sit overnight.

3 The next day, drain the liquid and toss the onions. Lightly pat the pork dry, and let it rest at room temperature for 1 hour. Transfer pork to roasting pan with rack.

4 Preheat the oven to broil setting. Broil the pork with fat side up for 15 minutes. Lower the oven temperature to 325°F, and continue cooking for 3½ to 4 hours, until thermometer inserted in the center reads 180°F. If the roast starts browning too much on top, tent the roast with foil.

5 Transfer the pork onto a carving board. Let it rest for 30 minutes before slicing.

1   Marinate the pork shoulder according to the same instructions. The next day, drain the liquid but keep the onions, and lightly pat the pork dry and let it rest at room temperature for 1 hour. Transfer pork to a roasting pan.

2   Preheat the oven to broil setting. Broil the pork with fat side up for 15 minutes. Lower the oven temperature to 325°F and continue cooking for 1 hour.

3   Take the pork out of the oven and add 2 cups of any liquid of your choice to the roasting pan; apple juice, broth, water or a combination work well.

4   Cover the pan tightly with foil and return to oven. Cook for another 2½ to 3 hours, until thermometer inserted in the center reads 205°F. Let pork rest for 30 minutes before shredding.

5   Mix the shredded pork with some of the juices from the roasting pan or your sauce of choice.

Chapter Eight

SCRAPPY

Pickled Veggies

Steamed Lettuce

Canned Ham Katsu

Chick Flavored Ramen

Easy "Steamed" Fish

Pecan Sticky Buns

Resourcefulness runs in my family and was passed down to me particularly by my maternal grandmother Popo (Amy Lili Chan, a.k.a. 婆婆, a.k.a. Popo), who is from the coastal city of Guangzhou in China. She is a woman who gets precisely what she's looking for, and uses it till it can be used no more. She's sharp, strategic and frugal. I lived with her for several years in grade school and watched her source her ingredients with unmatched strategy and single-mindedness.

Every week she made her rounds to the local grocery stores, getting the best deals on every single item she needed. Being raised in a coastal city, she was used to the best seafood, and she bought only live fish still flapping in a plastic bag to ensure freshness. She grew potato roots in jars and used eggshells for fertilizer rather than throwing them away. Everything could be used for something, and nothing went to waste. She even tore out pages of shopping catalogs sent to her house to discard seafood bones on at dinner instead of wasting napkins.

She owned a hen for more than a year, doting on it with devotion. She cleaned out its cage, prepared it special food, even gave it massages. She seemed truly smitten with the chicken. Each day the hen laid one egg. To Popo, each of those eggs was comparable to a golden ticket at the Willy Wonka factory. Then for a few weeks the hen stopped hatching eggs. It took a couple weeks to notice that the house was quieter—no more gobbling came from outside. I found out that my grandmother had killed the chicken. She had no qualms with detaching herself from what I had thought was her pet. In appreciation of the hen's life, she prepared us a variety of chicken dishes that week.

Her frugality ran deep in her bones, despite being wealthy later on in her life. She is a dedicated lifelong learner and is committed to sustainability. If she didn't know something, she would observe someone who did, or read books and start applying herself. She experimented with bread starters, jerky, wine, dehydrating fruit from her own trees and pickling vegetables from her garden. She wasn't above meals made in a dash, though. She embraced the convenience of the microwave, American canned foods and frozen dinners—even weekly fast-food runs. A typical dinner may have consisted of steamed lettuce with Spam and a small container of mashed potatoes from KFC. As a youngster, I thought we were eating like kings.

I started grocery shopping and preparing my lunches in fourth grade and did my own grocery shopping by fifth grade. Every Sunday evening, I walked to Lucky's and spent an hour or two roaming through the aisles, reading food labels and comparing prices. I never had a plan for what I would eat each week—it was more about getting the best bang for my buck from my allowance money. I have always been a freestyle cook, creating dishes around foods on sale or things I happened to have in the moment. It's a compelling challenge to whip up a meal out of leftovers. Watching Popo always use what is available taught me to see possibilities that aren't immediately apparent. I like to believe that anything is possible if you have the determination and creativity to make it happen. One of my favorite quotes is by Theodore Roosevelt, "Do what you can, with what you have, where you are." My grandmother exemplified this mantra, and I adopted it.

PICKLED VEGGIES

This is a universal pickling water that can be used for various vegetable combinations. Pickle veggies overnight and store in the fridge for up to three weeks in Mason jars or airtight containers.

MAKES 2 CUPS

1 cup white vinegar

1 cup water

¼ cup sugar

1 tablespoon salt

2 cups vegetables, such as cucumbers or carrots, sliced or chopped

1   In a small pot, combine vinegar, water, sugar and salt and bring to a boil.

2   Put vegetables into clean Mason jars. Pour pickling water into Mason jars over the vegetables and cool to room temperature.

3   Cover the jars and refrigerate overnight. It can be kept in the fridge for 3 weeks.

STEAMED LETTUCE

In Chinese culture, lettuce is typically served warm and saturated in oily pools of soy sauce or broth. I had eaten it only this way for years before I realized the rest of my peers only knew lettuce as a cold and crispy side. If you have never tried lettuce prepared this way, you may develop a craving for this vegetable dish.

SERVES 4

1 head iceberg lettuce

1 tablespoon vegetable oil

1 garlic clove, minced

1 teaspoon ginger, minced

2 teaspoons soy sauce

½ teaspoon sugar

¼ teaspoon white pepper

½ teaspoon salt

¼ cup water

1 tablespoon oyster sauce

1 tablespoon sesame oil

1   Separate the leaves of the head of lettuce but keep them whole.

2   In a wok or large pot, heat vegetable oil over medium-high heat. Add garlic and ginger, and cook until fragrant, about 30 seconds. Be careful not to burn. Add soy sauce, sugar, white pepper, salt and water.

3   Place leaves into pot in natural formation of the lettuce. Cover pot with a lid and let steam for 1 to 2 minutes, until the leaves are slightly wilted.

4   Place lettuce on a plate and add a drizzle of oyster sauce and sesame oil.

CANNED HAM KATSU

Popo loved Spam in a can. She swore that eating Spam, canned corn and a third helping of rice was healthy and would make us strong. I confess that Spam is a guilty pleasure of mine. Shallow fried and coated with a crust of panko bread crumbs, this recipe will make believers out of skeptics.

SERVES 4

6 eggs

1 cup panko bread crumbs

1 can Spam (sliced into 8 pieces, lengthwise)

3 tablespoons vegetable oil

2 cups cooked rice for serving

Chopped cilantro, for garnish

1 Prepare two shallow bowls. Beat 2 eggs in one bowl; put bread crumbs in the other. Dip the Spam slices into the eggs and then into bread crumbs until completely covered. Repeat for all the Spam slices.

2 Heat the oil in a pan over medium heat. Add the Spam slices and fry for 2 minutes on each side. Using chopsticks, flip Spam on the edges to get crispy all around.

3 Place fried Spam slices on a plate with a paper towel to absorb extra oil. Serve with rice and fried eggs, and garnish with chopped cilantro.

CHICK FLAVORED RAMEN

My grandmother Popo is one of the most complex women I know. She comes from the southern tip of China, where the cuisine shines thanks to the fresh ingredients, but at the same time she loves packaged and canned goods. One of her favorite tricks was making a quick packaged ramen and adding fresh ingredients. She's one of my inspirations when it comes to making these noodles.

SERVES 2

1 tablespoon sesame oil

1 tablespoon garlic, minced

1 jalapeño pepper, minced

3 tablespoons cilantro, chopped, plus more for serving

2 teaspoons ginger, minced

2 scallions, minced

1 teaspoon turmeric

2 packages chicken ramen noodles

1 cup white mushrooms, sliced

1 tomato, diced

1 (13.5-ounce) can coconut milk

1 lime, cut into wedges, for serving

1   In a medium pot, sauté sesame oil, garlic, jalapeño, cilantro, ginger, scallions and turmeric for 1 to 2 minutes on medium-low heat.

2   Add seasoning from the ramen noodle packet, then the mushrooms, and sauté until the mushrooms start to release their juices. Add tomato and coconut milk. Bring to a boil. Add ramen noodles and cook according to package instructions. Serve with lime wedges and fresh cilantro.

EASY "STEAMED" FISH

I am all about cutting corners in the kitchen. Microwaved tilapia is the epitome of cutting corners. It takes less than five minutes to make and it's a great source of protein. This is a great recipe to whip out if you want a nutritious meal but you're strapped for time.

SERVES 2

2 tilapia fillets

2 tablespoons ginger, cut into fine
  matchstick pieces

2 teaspoons soy sauce

2 teaspoons rice wine vinegar (mirin)

1 teaspoon sesame oil

½ teaspoon sugar

Cilantro or sliced scallions, for garnish

1   Place tilapia fillets in a microwave-safe, deep-sided dish.

2   In a small bowl, mix ginger, soy sauce, rice wine vinegar, sesame oil and sugar. Pour over the tilapia.

3   Cover the dish with plastic wrap and microwave for 2 to 3 minutes, until the fish is cooked through. Serve over rice and pickled veggies, and garnish with cilantro or scallions.

PECAN STICKY BUNS

My grandma is a self-starter. For as long as I can remember, she experimented in the kitchen. She made bread every few days, trying different proofing methods and amounts of yeast. The kitchen was her science lab. One of my fondest memories was waking up in the morning and smelling a cinnamon aroma in the air. These heavenly buns take me back to those days, though I'm just as happy using premade crescent roll dough today.

MAKES 12 ROLLS

½ cup brown sugar, packed

1 teaspoon cinnamon

1 teaspoon vanilla

½ cup butter, melted, divided

¾ cup chopped pecans

2 (8-ounce) containers of crescent dough

3 tablespoons honey

1. Preheat oven to 375°F. In a bowl, combine brown sugar, cinnamon and vanilla. Mix with fingers until well combined.

2. On a lightly floured surface, roll out both packages of crescent dough into one 21-by-8-inch rectangle, at about ¼-inch thickness. Brush ¼ cup of melted butter on the rectangle to cover. Reserve the remaining ¼ cup melted butter. Sprinkle ¼ cup packed brown sugar mixture over the butter. Top evenly with chopped pecans.

3. Starting lengthwise, roll dough up firmly into a log. Cut evenly into 12 pieces, about 1¾ inch for each piece. Lightly brush a 9-by-9-inch baking pan with some melted butter. Sprinkle the remaining brown sugar mixture in the pan, and then place rolls on top of the brown sugar, spacing evenly.

4. Bake rolls for 25 to 30 minutes, until golden brown and cooked through the center. Take rolls out of oven and let cool for 5 minutes. While rolls are still hot, carefully invert them onto a large plate, making sure all the melted brown sugar stays on top of the rolls. Drizzle the rolls with honey. Serve warm.

If you could eat only one food for the rest of your life, what would it be? Without hesitation, I would choose eggs. They have been by far the most loyal in the kitchen and the foundation of my culinary journey. Like all great loves, my lifelong relationship with eggs has had its ups and downs.

The egg is and always has been a staple in my kitchen. When I was younger, my mom, who took little joy in cooking, loved making scrambled eggs: easy, quick, done. The trouble was she didn't exactly have a plan for what style of egg she would be cooking. She cranked the heat up high, cracked the shell open and would fold or flip or prod till it was edible. Scrambled? Damaged sunny-side up? Attempted over easy with burned edges?

Aside from the scrambled eggs, other dubious versions that were familiar to me were pungent preserved duck eggs served with rice and veggies, or desserts with an egg flavor: steamed eggs or the sweet, flaky egg tarts made with pork lard at dim sum. Not to mention all the church potlucks, where gallons of gloppy mayo infiltrated the egg and potato salads usually dominating a large table. The stench of hundreds of exposed eggs always caused me to cover my nose.

When I began to cook for myself, I realized how crucial the egg is to the cook. It has the power to hold everything together and has been my personal lifesaver. Although I had a bad first impression of eggs, my appreciation for these plain, oval beauties grew as I began to see how truly versatile they are.

Many of my revolting experiences with eggs were due to the way they had been prepared, which could have been easily fixed. For example, a change in technique could produce a luxurious soufflé-style omelet with the same ingredients my mom had used to scramble.

A veggie omelet is made with chopped vegetables and a few fried eggs; whereas the shakshuka is poached eggs simmered inside a tomato stew and flavored with salt and pepper. The taste of a food comes from the method rather than the food itself.

When considering cuisines around the world, the simple egg can be unrecognizable in all its various forms. A no-frills, rolled omelet makes the classic French style. In Japan, egg is rolled into a sweet and custardy log and put on a stick, called *tamagoyaki*. The Korean *gyeran-jjim* is a savory dish of eggs whisked and then steamed to create a silky-smooth texture, and topped with onions and sesame seeds. China is known for its black Century egg (a special method of preserving), a common snack and pantry staple that dates back hundreds of years and is an acquired taste. Thailand serves the *khai jiao*: an omelet soft on the inside with a golden crispy outside. The Portuguese Pastel de nata is a tart with a sweet egg custard center surrounded by a flaky crust.

During a visit to Germany, I tried Frankfurt Green Sauce. This is a traditional German spread made of boiled eggs, sour cream and herbs. While going to make a snack for myself, I found a deep tray of a creamy green sauce with herbs. Without knowing what it was, but enticed by the color and novelty, I spread it on a piece of toasted pumpernickel bread and topped it with tomato and cucumber slices. My friend, her German boyfriend and I canceled our dinner reservation that evening, only to finish the last of the green sauce instead.

While the egg may have been a villain in most of my meals as a youngster, today I can't live without it. There are about a million and one ways to prepare an egg. Before I realized this, I was working against and not with it.

FLUFFY EGGS

This is as fluffy as it gets! By whipping the egg whites and later folding the yolks back in, you get the fluffiest eggs ever. You can add fresh herbs or eat it scrambled. Say good-bye to rubbery eggs.

SERVES 2

6 eggs

2 tablespoons heavy cream

Salt and pepper, to taste

1 tablespoon butter

1   Separate the egg whites and yolks into two separate bowls. Using an electric mixer, beat egg whites until they form soft, airy peaks.

2   Beat the egg yolks and a splash of heavy cream. Season yolks with salt and pepper. Fold yolks into the egg whites.

3   On medium-low heat, add butter and melt, and then add the egg mixture. Let the eggs cook slightly before making gentle folds until the egg is slightly cooked and wet. Remove from heat and serve.

CHORIZO & EGGS

You've never had a chorizo and egg breakfast dish like this one. The red oil from the sausage soaks through the scrambled eggs, making every bite moist and flavorful. Top with sour cream and you've got a meal your taste buds won't forget.

SERVES 2

½ medium onion, chopped

¼ pound fresh Mexican chorizo, casings removed

6 large eggs

Salt and black pepper

Cilantro, for garnish

Tortillas, for serving

1 In a medium skillet, sauté chorizo and onions over medium heat until browned and cooked through.

2 Beat eggs with salt and pepper in a bowl and pour into skillet on top of the chorizo. Gently fold the eggs into the chorizo and cook until eggs are soft and still slightly wet. Remove from heat. Garnish with cilantro and serve with tortillas.

STOVE-TOP SHAKSHUKA

This poached egg recipe looks fancy but is deceptively simple. The eggs are nestled and poached inside the spiced tomato stew. It can be conveniently eaten straight from the pan. Best served with a crusty bread.

SERVES 2

1 tablespoon olive oil

¼ cup onion, diced

¼ cup bell pepper, diced

1 garlic clove, minced

Pinch of red pepper flakes

1 (18-ounce) can tomatoes, crushed

2 tablespoons tomato paste

¼ teaspoon paprika

¼ teaspoon cumin

1 teaspoon sugar

Salt and black pepper, to taste

2 eggs

Chopped parsley, for garnish

Feta, for serving (optional)

Crusty bread, for serving

1   In a large pan, heat oil over medium-high heat. Add onion, bell pepper, garlic and red pepper flakes. Cook until vegetables are translucent, about 3 minutes.

2   Add crushed tomatoes, tomato paste, paprika, cumin and sugar. Bring to a simmer. Reduce heat slightly, and simmer for about 10 minutes.

3   Season to taste with salt and pepper. When sauce becomes slightly thicker, make two small wells, and crack an egg into each well. Simmer eggs until the whites of the eggs are cooked through, but the yolks are still runny. Remove from heat, top with parsley and feta, and serve from the pan with crusty bread.

RED DEVILED EGGS

Deviled eggs were originally named for their zesty or spicy flavor. While they have become lackluster at most potlucks, I think they should be more devilish in appearance. These are topped with chives for extra frehsness. One bite and you may become possessed— I mean obsessed.

SERVES 4

12 large hard-boiled eggs, peeled

2 teaspoons mustard

3 tablespoons mayonnaise

1 tablespoon lemon juice

3 tablespoons finely chopped
   sun-dried tomatoes in olive oil

Salt, to taste

Cracked black pepper, to taste

1 teaspoon of olive oil from
   sun-dried tomatoes

1 tablespoon snipped fresh chives

1   Using a sharp knife, slice the eggs in half and gently remove the yolks.

2   With a fork, mash the yolks, mustard, mayo and lemon juice, until mixture is smooth. Fold in the chopped sun-dried tomatoes. Season to taste with salt and black pepper.

3   Place mixture in a ziplock bag and snip a corner of the bag. Squeeze mixture into egg white halves. Drizzle the sun-dried tomato oil on top of the eggs. Sprinkle with chopped chives.

FRANKFURT GREEN EGGS

This green sauce is a popular dish from Frankfurt, Germany. It is made with hard-boiled eggs, sour cream and a host of herbs. I first tried it on a slice of toasted pumpernickel bread and was so swept off my feet I canceled my dinner plans to finish off this delectable treat. It is traditionally served over boiled potatoes and hard-boiled eggs but can also be served as a dip.

SERVES 6

4 hard-boiled eggs, peeled, plus
   more for serving

1 tablespoon lemon juice

2 tablespoons olive oil

¼ cup sour cream

1 cup plain whole-milk yogurt

½ to 1 cup of each of the following herbs
   for a total of 2 cups: chives, garden
   cress, parsley

Salt and black pepper, to taste

12–18 small white boiled potatoes
   peeled, for serving (optional)

1   Slice the 4 hard-boiled eggs in half. Set aside the egg whites and mix the egg yolks in a small bowl with the lemon juice, olive oil, sour cream and yogurt.

2   In a food processor, pulse the herbs, scraping down the sides of bowl after every few pulses, until the herbs are bright green and finely chopped.

3   Add the egg-yolk mixture, and process until it comes together into a green sauce consistency. Add the egg whites and pulse the food processor until the egg whites are just finely chopped, but don't overprocess. The egg whites will slightly thicken the sauce and give it some texture.

4   Remove the green sauce from the food processor into a bowl and season to taste with plenty of salt and freshly ground black pepper. Eggs love salt and pepper. Serve with slices of hard-boiled egg and boiled potatoes.

SWEET & TANGY EGG SALAD

I've never been thrilled by traditional egg salad with mayo. To give the egg salad some pizzazz, I make my own mixture, which includes oil, mustard and honey. Add a dash of cracked pepper and salt, and you've got a new-and-improved egg salad!

SERVES 2

4 hard-boiled eggs, peeled

2 tablespoons olive oil

½ teaspoon honey

1 teaspoon mustard

Cracked sea salt

Cracked black pepper

2 dashes hot sauce

4 slices crustless white bread

Edible flowers, for garnish

1   Grate the hard-boiled eggs into chunks.

2   In a bowl, mix the eggs with olive oil, honey and mustard. Add cracked sea salt and black pepper. Add a dash or two of hot sauce to taste, and gently blend.

3   Spread the mixture between slices of bread. Cut each sandwich in half, and garnish with edible flowers.

Chapter Ten

CANTONESE

Jook

Hong Kong–Style Borscht

Microwave "Steamed" Eggs

Cola Chicken Wings

Baked Macau-Style Portuguese Chicken

Chia Mango Pudding

In a Cantonese family, food is at the center of every family meeting. My paternal grandmother "Mama" (a.k.a. Rosanna Mui, a.k.a. 嫲嫲) planned all our activities around meals. Each one was more excessive than the last, and always required takeout boxes at the end. In fact, we were never able to eat everything; to her, abundance looked like a table filled with leftovers after the guests are happily full. Feeding people around the table is her pride and joy. She would probably invent holidays if it were up to her. She was the first "foodie" I knew.

At a young age, I was exposed to all sorts of bizarre dishes: congee, a Chinese rice porridge made with chicken liver, savory braised grapefruit skins, chicken feet and fermented duck eggs. Cantonese food is one of the most extraordinary cuisines in the world, involving a wide range of cooking techniques and a variety of commonly discarded animal products transformed into delicacies.

All the recipes my grandma has ever made have been etched into her mind as though it were a stone. She can recite every ingredient and direction to a tee. Her cooking philosophy is simple: You get what you put in. Cooking was sacred to her. She would never dream of being impatient or skimping on quality of products. For example, she would roll up to a Chinese herbal store and pay a pretty penny for dried abalone and ginseng.

She taught me the different flavor profiles: sweet, bitter, tart, salty and spicy, and how to balance them to create the perfect dish. She took pride in her refined palate, making no reservations about vocalizing her opinions. Once while we ate our typical weekend dim sum lunch, she unapologetically critiqued each dish—to us and to the waitstaff. She had no qualms about dissecting what was superb or subpar about what she ate. Being a frequent patron at Cantonese restaurants in the San Francisco Bay Area, she still has a way of leveraging her influence by getting the tables with the best locations without a wait.

It was only recently that Mama shared her struggle for survival in adolescence with me, giving me insight into why she frequently tells me I am too skinny and that I need to eat more. She was born prematurely in the Macao region of southern China, and her parents deemed her a lost cause at birth. Her uncle and aunt unofficially adopted her after not being able to have children of their own, and she became their pride and joy. Her uncle fattened her with a constant supply of milk, despite its expense, and she grew to be a healthy and chubby girl. He bought her a prized jade bracelet, a symbol in Chinese culture of safety and health. However, when her own parents saw how she had blossomed into a healthy child, they wanted her back. She did not want to return to them but had no choice.

In her early life, eating was so much more than mere enjoyment—it was survival. Later on, she ended up coming to her uncle's rescue as he had come to hers. He was struggling and she brought him a constant supply of rice and clothing from her home. She believed that life comes full circle: Her uncle saved her early in her life when she needed help and she was able to help him when he needed it. It is our duty to do good to others, as it returns to us eventually.

My grandmother never finished middle school and was ridden with insecurity about her lack of education. Later in life, when her kids were in school, in between her Mahjong and Chinese opera events, she went to a local cooking school to better herself. At that point, she was living a well-to-do life, with two full-time nannies. My grandmother was a woman who lived life on both sides of the tracks. She jokes now that at this point in her life, all she cares about is eating well.

JOOK

Jook is a rice porridge. Every Chinese household has its own recipe and the consistency varies according to each cook's personal style. This is one of my mom's remedies for any sickness. A good jook should be creamy, with the rice grains mostly dissolved into the soup. My grandmother's secret to good jook is to marinate the rice with sesame oil the night before so it blends easily after cooking. As long as you marinate the rice, you can cook the jook in a pot, slow cooker or rice cooker.

SERVES 6

½ cup jasmine rice

1 tablespoon sesame oil

½ teaspoon white pepper

1 teaspoon kosher salt

5 cups water

1-inch piece ginger

2 boneless, skinless chicken thighs

1 tablespoon of cilantro, finely chopped

1 scallion, finely chopped

1 preserved egg, chopped (optional), found in many Asian markets

1   The day before: Marinate rice in sesame oil, white pepper and salt.

2   The next day, place the marinated rice in a large pot on the stove-top. Add water, ginger and chicken. Bring to a simmer, and cook until the grains are soft and translucent, about 1 hour.

3   Turn off the heat and take the chicken out of the pot. When it has cooled slightly, shred the chicken and add it back into the pot. Season to taste with salt and pepper.

4   To serve, ladle into bowls and garnish with sliced scallions, cilantro, ginger and sesame oil. Garnishing with a preserved egg is optional.

HONG KONG-STYLE BORSCHT

Hong Kong cuisine is best explained as the merging of Eastern and Western flavors, and has variations on Western dishes. My grandmother lived in Hong Kong for more than half her life. This is where she learned how to cook. This Hong Kong spin on a traditional Russian dish is a slightly sweet beef broth with veggies—a satisfying comfort food.

SERVES 6

1 pound veal oxtail or beef shank

1 teaspoon salt, divided

1 teaspoon black pepper, divided

3 tablespoons vegetable oil, divided

8 cups water

1 onion, diced

3 garlic cloves, minced

3 carrots, peeled and cut into
   1-inch pieces

3 celery stalks, sliced

½ cabbage, roughly chopped

1 potato, peeled and diced

3 tablespoons tomato paste

1 (16-ounce) can diced tomatoes

1 tablespoon lemon juice

2 tablespoons Worcestershire sauce

½ cup ketchup

1. Season oxtails or beef shank generously with salt and pepper.

2. Heat 2 tablespoons oil in a large pot or Dutch oven over medium-high heat. Sear the oxtails until golden brown and caramelized on all sides.

3. Add the water to the pot. Bring to a simmer and cook the oxtails for 2½ to 3 hours until the meat is tender. Skim and discard any scum that surfaces.

4. Next, add the onion, garlic, carrots, celery, cabbage and potato to the soup, and cook for another 30 minutes.

5. Add tomato paste, diced tomatoes, lemon juice, Worcestershire sauce and ketchup. Cook for another 30 minutes, until oxtails are tender and vegetables are soft. Season with salt and black pepper, to taste, and serve.

MICROWAVE "STEAMED" EGGS

These are my grandma's unforgettable steamed eggs. Never fear: If you are pressed for time in the morning, I find using a microwave instead of a steamer still makes a delicious breakfast.

SERVES 2

2 room-temperature eggs (reserve shells)

Water

Pinch of salt and white pepper

1 teaspoon sesame oil, plus more
  for serving

1 teaspoon soy sauce

Sliced scallions, for garnish

1   Crack two fresh eggs into a microwave-safe bowl. Fill each eggshell with cold water and pour water into bowl. Whip eggs and water with a fork.

2   Add a pinch of salt and white pepper. Gently blend in sesame oil. Cover bowl with plastic wrap. Heat in the microwave for 2 minutes.

3   Drizzle eggs with sesame oil and soy sauce, and garnish with scallions. Serve over rice.

COLA CHICKEN WINGS

My grandmother's recipes are all in her head, from the ingredient measurements to the temperature of the stove-top. She says that there is one specific way to make this recipe, but I beg to differ. This is her recipe but with an added dose of creativity.

MAKES 6 LARGE CHICKEN WINGS

GRANDMA'S VERSION

⅓ cup Chinese rose wine

2 cups dark soy sauce

1 12-ounce can Coca-Cola

2 teaspoons MSG (optional)

2 pounds large chicken wings

1   In a medium pot, boil wine, soy sauce, Coca-Cola and MSG together. Add wings and cook for 8 to 10 minutes.

2   Turn off immediately after cooking time and let chicken soak for 10 minutes with a lid on. Serve as an appetizer.

MY VERSION

2 pounds large chicken wings

3 tablespoons oil

3 ¼-inch slices of ginger

2 teaspoons Chinese rose wine

3 tablespoons soy sauce

1 cup Coca-Cola (room temperature)

1 star anise

Chopped scallions, for garnish

1   In a medium pan, sear chicken wings over medium-high heat in the oil. Add ginger and cook until slightly golden, about 2 to 3 minutes.

2   Add Chinese rose wine, soy sauce, Coca-Cola and star anise. Cook chicken wings with lid on for 10 minutes on medium-low heat. Serve as an appetizer, garnished with scallions.

BAKED MACAU-STYLE
PORTUGUESE CHICKEN

This recipe has three parts: chicken, sauce and egg fried rice. My paternal grandmother was born in Macau, a Portuguese colony in Southern China, and she makes a very flavorful Portuguese chicken over rice. Egg fried rice and crispy chicken bits float in a delicious broth flavored with turmeric. The broiled cheese on top takes it to the next level. I have many fond memories of eating this in Hong Kong cafés with my father and brother when I was younger.

CHICKEN

1 pound boneless, skinless chicken thighs
   (cut into 1-inch pieces)

1 tablespoon + 1 teaspoon cornstarch, divided

1 tablespoon soy sauce

½ teaspoon salt

¼ teaspoon ground white pepper

1 medium potato (peeled and cut into
   ¾-inch cubes)

3 tablespoons vegetable oil

SAUCE

½ cup onion, minced

2 garlic cloves, minced

1 teaspoon ginger, grated

1 teaspoon curry powder

½ teaspoon turmeric

1 tablespoon unsweetened coconut flakes,
   plus more for serving

1 13.5-ounce can coconut milk

RICE

2 tablespoons sesame oil

3 eggs, beaten

4 cups leftover cooked jasmine rice

Salt and white pepper, to taste

½ cup mozzarella cheese, shredded

1   In a bowl, mix together the chicken, 1 tablespoon cornstarch, soy sauce, salt and white pepper. Set aside for 5 minutes.

2   In a large skillet over medium heat, sauté chicken and potato cubes in 2 tablespoons oil until slightly golden brown. Remove chicken and potatoes from pan.

3   In the same pan over medium heat, add the rest of the oil and sauté onions with garlic, ginger, curry powder, turmeric and unsweetened coconut flakes. When onions have become translucent and fragrant, add coconut milk and bring to a simmer.

4   Add the chicken and potatoes back into the pan.

5   In a small bowl, mix 1 teaspoon cornstarch with a few teaspoons of the simmering sauce. Pour cornstarch mixture back into pan and continue to simmer until the sauce has thickened and reduced, potatoes have softened, and the chicken is cooked through, about 15 minutes.

6   Over medium heat, heat 2 tablespoons sesame oil in a wok or large skillet. Add eggs and fold gently. Once eggs are scrambled, add rice. Gently fold egg into the rice. Season rice with salt and white pepper.

7   Set oven to broil. Place egg rice into casserole dish. Spoon sauce all over top of rice. Sprinkle cheese and unsweetened coconut flakes. Place casserole in oven and broil for 3 minutes, until cheese is bubbly and golden brown.

CHIA MANGO PUDDING

My grandma made stellar mango pudding that resembled Jell-O. This sweet pudding is made with overnight-soaked chia seeds and has a creamy texture, one that even granny would approve of.

SERVES 4

½ cup chia seeds

¼ cup sweetened condensed milk

2 cups coconut milk

1 large mango, cut into ½-inch cubes

1 In a medium bowl, cover the chia seeds with sweetened condensed milk and coconut milk and refrigerate overnight.

2 The next day, give the chia seeds a stir to smooth out clumps. Serve either chilled or warm, topped with fresh mango.

Chapter Eleven

MOTHERLAND

Dumplings

Microwaved "Steamed" Tofu

Spicy Cold Korean Noodles

Pork Belly Over Rice

Poblano Chicken Stir-Fry

Jajangmyeon Noodles

To go anywhere in the world, all you need is the will and two suitcases. I spent a year in Shanghai in 2015 as part of my graduate program for international studies. The first part was exhilarating yet stressful. I lived in a studio apartment on a teacher's salary. I had to be frugal and resourceful, with no oven, tiny burners and a mini fridge. No one was going to catch me if I fell. It dawned on me there that I had been preparing for this experience my entire life. My childhood was spent watching my mother scrape resources together from the little we had, and all my experimenting in the kitchen was needed now more than ever.

Eating on a budget led me to venture out to local open markets. Anything goes in China, it would seem, and I was in a constant state of fascination mixed with trepidation. Whatever you desired was at the market: produce, hand-pulled noodles, half a pig sliced at the customer's request. The butcher who sliced my pork would place my change on the same cutting board that had been dampened with pig blood. Locals plucked chicken feathers and snapped frog legs on the street. This was the dizzying norm, and it was jarring to say the least. My friends in the program and I coined the phrase "when in China," to describe the flexibility needed to adapt to an unpredictable environment.

I attempted to cook the food I tried on the street in my own kitchen, yet the meal that required the most improvisation was carnitas. I had joined a community expat group for people living abroad, and at one point we were craving Mexican food. I volunteered to make a taco bar for everyone, even though tacos aren't the easiest meal to assemble from local Chinese markets.

I have always been of the mind-set of asking for forgiveness, not permission. I don't say if, I ask how. I was going to make carnitas from Chinese open markets. Pork shoulder can be stewed in a rice cooker and the pork juices can be used for orange rice. "Black beans" can be made out of Chinese red beans and flavored with Xi'an spices and fresh cilantro.

It may not have been easy to pull off, but such a small victory as making Mexican food in Shanghai showed that limitation can be a launching pad for creativity.

Dining etiquette in China was not only vastly different than Western norms, but also opened my eyes to my own roots. In college, I overheard a girl commenting to my roommates about her annoyance with my slurping when I ate. Yet in China, slurping is the way noodles are eaten. Personal space in restaurants was not a concept. In a culture where practicality trumps propriety, joining a stranger at her table because the restaurant is busy is not given a second thought. These incidents made me understand why I had butted heads with my family. I didn't understand their upbringing. Now I was finally becoming proud that I had come from a long line of resourceful people.

Throughout my entire life, I had never felt fully Chinese or fully American. A gap stood between these two parts that I couldn't bridge. I didn't understand my family's history and upbringing within the context of my own largely Western experience. I lived disjointed, not knowing exactly what wasn't in its place. Not being able to reconcile these parallel parts of my life, I felt out of sync, and I resented it.

However, the immersion into an Eastern mind-set made me understand that our life experience is based largely on our interpretation of it. The concept that one way of life was either right or wrong, better or worse than another did not exist. I didn't need to be more Chinese or more American. There was no conflict. I see the world uniquely because of being Chinese American. In China, a culture where seemingly anything goes, my ideals of what I should be evaporated, along with the persona that had accompanied them. I have traded in my demands for the life I thought I was supposed to have been born into, and instead I'm embracing the integration of two in one. Across oceans, I came home.

DUMPLINGS

The excitement of trying new foods wore off about a month and a half into my time living in Shanghai. I missed home and craved a familiar comfort food. I walked by the market every week and saw all the ingredients for dumplings, so I bought what I remembered my mom used in them when I was just five years old. Surprisingly, that powerful memory helped me make the exact dumplings she did.

DIPPING SAUCE

4 tablespoons soy sauce

2 tablespoons hot water

2 teaspoons rice wine vinegar

2 teaspoons sesame oil

2 teaspoons sugar

2 teaspoons ginger, grated

4 cloves garlic, grated

1 whole scallion, sliced

1 small red chili, minced, or a pinch of red chili flakes

DUMPLINGS

1 pound ground pork (20-25% fat, found at Asian markets)

2 tablespoons sesame oil

2 tablespoons soy sauce

1 teaspoon ginger, grated

3 garlic cloves, minced

1 cup napa cabbage, shredded

2 scallions, finely sliced

1 teaspoon rice wine vinegar

1 teaspoon cornstarch

1 egg

¾ teaspoon salt

½ teaspoon white pepper

50 circular dumpling wrappers

1   Mix all dipping sauce ingredients in a bowl. Set aside while you make the dumplings.

2   In a large mixing bowl, add all dumpling ingredients except the wrappers and mix by hand until combined.

3   Spoon 1 tablespoon dumpling filling in the center of the dumpling wrapper. Do not overfill, making sure there is room around the edges to enclose the dumpling.

4   Using your finger, wet the edges of the dumpling wrapper, fold in half, pinching the edges together, creating a half-moon and then folding 3 to 4 pleats along the edge of the wrapper.

5   Place finished dumplings onto a lightly floured surface. Repeat with the remaining filling and wrappers until all the filing is used.

6   To cook dumplings, bring a large pot of water to a boil and gently place them in water, without overcrowding the pot. You may need to cook dumplings in several batches. Keep dumplings from sticking to the bottom of the pot by gently nudging them with a spoon as they cook.

7   Simmer until dumplings float and are cooked through the center, about 3 to 4 minutes. Using a slotted spoon, remove the dumplings to a plate. Continue cooking the rest of the dumplings in batches.

8   Serve hot dumplings with dipping sauce.

MICROWAVED "STEAMED" TOFU

This is a vegetarian rendition of steamed fish. It's a convenient option if cooking for one, as I frequently was while in China. Tofu is always a great staple when you're looking for something light and nutritious.

SERVES 4

1 (12-ounce) package soft tofu, cut into 4 rectangles

1 2-inch piece ginger, peeled and thinly sliced into matchstick shapes

1 scallion, thinly sliced

1 garlic clove, minced

1 teaspoon Chinese cooking wine

1 teaspoon honey

2 tablespoons vegetable oil

Pinch red pepper flakes

1   Place tofu in a microwaveable glass dish.

2   In a small bowl, mix all ingredients together. Pour sauce on top of tofu and cover the dish with plastic wrap. Microwave for 3 minutes. Serve over white rice.

SPICY COLD
KOREAN NOODLES

Korean *Bibim Naengmyeon* is an icy noodle in a vinegar broth with sweet and spicy hot sauce, topped with sliced beef, half a boiled egg and a tower of thinly grated cucumbers and pears. This dish has many different components, so it takes time to prepare. Although it's tempting to cook every component myself, I pride myself on deconstructing recipes to make it easy for the everyday person. This is a great recipe to prepare ahead of time and can be a go-to meal prep dish.

SERVES 2

8 ounces Asian noodles

2 tablespoons sesame oil

6 tablespoons gochujang paste

2 tablespoons soy sauce

2 tablespoons apple cider vinegar

1 medium Asian pear, peeled and pureed in a blender

1 Asian pear, thinly sliced, for serving

1 cucumber, julienned, for serving

2 soft-boiled eggs, peeled and halved, for serving

Toasted sesame seeds, for serving

1 teaspoon Chinese cooking wine

1 teaspoon honey

2 tablespoons vegetable oil

Pinch red pepper flakes

1   Cook noodles according to package instructions. When noodles are done cooking, shock them in a bowl of ice water to chill completely.

2   In a medium bowl, combine sesame oil, gochujang paste, soy sauce, apple cider vinegar and pureed pear.

3   To serve, divide noodles into two bowls, and add a generous spoonful of sauce. Garnish with the sliced pear, cucumber and sesame seeds, and top each bowl with a hard-boiled egg.

PORK BELLY OVER RICE

Since I'm Chinese, it's my default to love pork and eggs together. I love the way the sweetness of the soy sauce covers the pork and rice like syrup. The crispy pork fat is perhaps the best part of this dish. I found many variations of this in China, all delicious in their own way. Here is my version of this classic Chinese dish.

SERVES 4

1 pound pork belly (sliced ⅓-inch pieces)

Salt and black pepper, to taste

2 portobello mushrooms, sliced

2 garlic cloves, minced

1 shallot, minced

1 tablespoon ginger, minced

1 teaspoon Chinese five-spice powder

2 tablespoons sugar

1 tablespoon rice wine vinegar

3 tablespoons dark soy sauce

1 bay leaf

4 eggs, for serving

Soy Sauce Eggs (see page 18)

Chopped scallions, for garnish

Steamed bok choy (optional)

1   In a large sauté pan over medium-low heat, add pork belly in a single layer. Add a pinch of salt and pepper. Let pork belly get golden brown and caramelized all over, about 10 to 15 minutes.

2   Turn down the heat as needed to keep the fat from splattering. Spoon out some of the fat from the pan and discard or save for another use, leaving about 3 tablespoons in the pan.

3   Add the mushrooms, and sauté for about 1 minute.

4   Add garlic, shallots and ginger, and sauté until fragrant, about 1 more minute. Add Chinese five-spice powder, sugar, rice wine vinegar, soy sauce and bay leaf. Simmer on medium-low, stirring as needed.

5   Serve pork belly and sauce in a bowl of rice topped with an egg and scallions.

POBLANO
CHICKEN STIR-FRY

The woman I bought my produce from in Shanghai would always sneak a few free peppers into my grocery bag, which got me experimenting with peppers in the kitchen. I deseeded poblano peppers but feel free to add the seeds for an extra kick. This recipe has a slurry mixture, a classic thickener found in Chinese sauces, that coats the rice grains. I made this all the time in China since it is delicious, affordable and easy to make!

SERVES 2

2 tablespoons sesame oil

2 garlic cloves, minced

2 boneless, skinless chicken thighs, cut into ¾-inch pieces

1 whole poblano pepper, deseeded (¾-inch cubes)

1 teaspoon sugar

2 tablespoons soy sauce

1 teaspoon rice wine vinegar

½ teaspoon cornstarch

2 teaspoons water

Salt and black pepper, to taste

1   In a wok or large pan over medium heat, heat 2 teaspoons sesame oil and sauté garlic. Add chicken and fry until golden brown.

2   Add poblano pepper and sauté until softened. Add sugar, soy sauce and rice wine vinegar.

3   In a small bowl, mix cornstarch with water until smooth. Add cornstarch slurry into stir-fry. Season with salt and black pepper. Serve over rice.

JAJANGMYEON NOODLES

I first tried these noodles at a food court in a Korean supermarket, and instantly fell in love. Imagine this: thick chunks of crispy pork morsels hiding in a gooey black bean ragu sauce filled with veggies and sitting on top of a bed of hand-pulled chewy noodles. Although traditionally a Korean dish, these noodles are widely served in China as well. I highly recommend going to your local Asian grocery store for the egg noodles and black bean sauce for the most authentic rendition.

SERVES 4

1 teaspoon ginger, minced

1 tablespoon garlic, minced

2 tablespoons sesame oil

8 ounces pork belly, cut into
  ½-inch pieces

1 potato, peeled and diced

½ cup onions, diced

½ cup carrots, diced

1 medium zucchini, diced

1 tablespoon sugar

2 tablespoons rice wine vinegar

6 tablespoons Korean black bean paste

1 cup starch water from noodles

1 cup chicken stock

1 teaspoon cornstarch

16 ounces cooked Korean wheat noodles,
  for serving

1 cucumber, julienned, for serving

Sesame seeds, for garnish

1   In a medium-size pot, sauté ginger and garlic over medium heat in sesame oil. Add pork belly chunks and sauté until browned for about 5 to 7 minutes.

2   Add potato, onion, carrot and zucchini, and stir-fry for 3 to 4 minutes.

3   Add sugar, rice wine vinegar, black bean paste, starch, water and chicken stock and simmer until it reduces by about half.

4   Mix cornstarch with a few teaspoons of water in a separate small bowl until smooth, then pour it into the sauce. Cook sauce until it coats the back of a spoon. Serve over wheat noodles and garnish with cucumber and sesame seeds.

DIY CHARCUTERIE BOARD

Stick to the three Cs for creating a charcuterie board and you will be the hostess with the mostest at your next gathering.

COMPONENTS

CHEESES

Pick one of each type of cheese
(factor in 3 to 4 ounces total cheese per guest)

Creamy: Brie, Camembert, goat cheese

Aged: Gouda, cheddar

Firm: Parmigiano-Reggiano

Blue: Gorgonzola

SPREADS & DIPS

Pesto

Olive oil & vinegar

Sun-Dried Tomato Pesto Dip

Marmalade & jams

MEATS

Prosciutto

Salami

CARBS

Breads

Crackers

ADDITIONS

Dried fruits

Fresh fruit & berries

CURATING

Let cheese sit at room temperature for an hour before arranging. Place cheese first onto the center of a tray or plate. Add accompanied components surrounding the cheese. Use labels for each cheese. Set out cheese knives for guests to cut their own slices.

COLOR

Pick a color scheme or season as an inspiration, and pick platters that are suitable to theme (e.g., wood planks, iron platters). Contrast colors together: golden honeycomb on top of blue cheese.

OPTIONAL

Add sprigs of herbs and/or edible flowers

EVERYDAY DRINKS

My mother served this drink to my brother and me when we were young as a preventative remedy for colds and sore throats. I have grown so accustomed to this drink for its comforting and refreshing quality, I make it as a treat.

1 cup (8 ounces) hot water

2 lemon slices

1 tablespoon pure honey

Place lemon slices and honey into a mug. Using a fork, press on the lemon slices to squeeze out some juice. Pour the hot water into the mug. Mix until the honey dissolves. Let sit for 1 to 2 minutes before serving.

MICROWAVED MOCHA

SERVES 1

This is my favorite way to start the morning. Melt a few pieces of chocolate you have in your cabinet for an instantly yummier coffee.

1½ ounces chocolate bar or chips

1 cup freshly brewed hot coffee

2 tablespoons half-and-half

Place the chocolate bar or chips into a mug. Pour hot coffee over the chocolate and mix with a spoon until chocolate dissolves. Add the half-and-half and serve.

MELTING POT

No need to buy expensive fresh juices. The Green Gingy Smoothie is filled with a helping of greens, apple and a bit of ginger for a kick. Chill ingredients before juicing for best juice. Enjoy!

½ cup fresh or frozen spinach

1 medium apple, peeled, cored and sliced

1¼-inch slice fresh ginger, peeled

1 tablespoon lemon juice

½ cup of citrus juice, such as orange or grapefruit juice

Place the spinach, apples, ginger, lemon juice and citrus juice into a blender. Blend on high until smooth. Add 1 to 2 tablespoon of extra citrus juice to adjust consistency, if needed. Serve in a Mason jar or glass.

PARTY DRINKS

SANGRIA

SERVES 8

Sangria is a wonderful drink that can be customized to the preferences of its maker. It can be made with either red or white wine, and your favorite fruit combination. (One type of citrus fruit is recommended for best taste.) Allow the fruit to marinate in the wine overnight. Enjoy at your next shower or party!

1 750-milliliter bottle white or red wine

2 tablespoons white sugar

1 cup citrus juice, such as orange juice

1 cup fruit, sliced, such as oranges, apples, lemons, limes

2 cups ginger ale

Combine wine, sugar and citrus juice in a large pitcher or pot. Mix until the sugar dissolves. Add the fruit. Let the mixture chill for 4 hours. Remove from the refrigerator and add the ginger ale. Serve in glasses.

MIMOSA

SERVES 8

This popular and tasty drink contains only two ingredients. Mimosa is three parts chilled sparkling champagne to one part citrus juice. Although the fruit can vary, it is traditionally garnished with cherries and strawberries. Brunch, anyone?

1 750-milliliter bottle dry Champagne or other sparkling wine, chilled

1 to 1½ cups fresh-squeezed orange juice

Fresh cherries and strawberries, to garnish

Fill Champagne flutes ¼ full with fresh-squeezed orange juice. Top the rest of the flute with Champagne. Add a garnish to each Champagne flute.

GAME PLAN MENUS

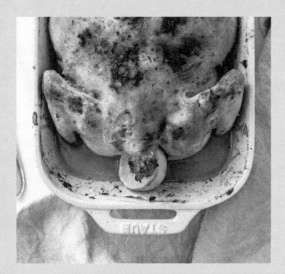

MAMA'S ESSENTIAL
KITCHEN KIT

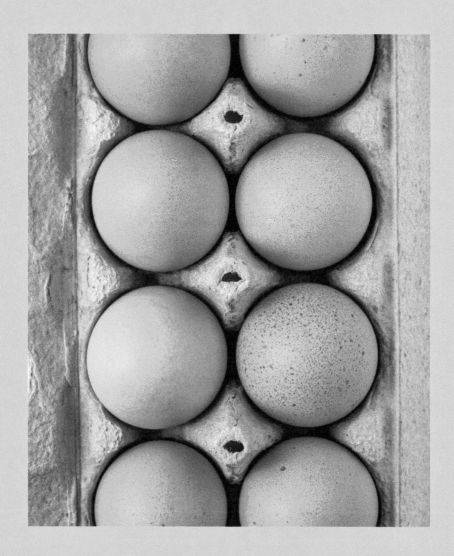

Appliances

FOOD PROCESSOR

A food processor can be used in more ways than you can imagine. Whether you're dicing or shredding vegetables or grinding meat, this appliance is going to save you a world of time in the kitchen. Some models even knead dough and make juice. Use it to your full advantage!

BLENDER

Great for making sauces or smoothies.

SLOW COOKER

This was my mom's favorite appliance in the kitchen due to the "set it and forget it" method. For those who want wholesome, luxurious meals with little effort, this is a must-have.

RICE COOKER

Whether you plan to make rice for one or a large quantity, a rice cooker is the most convenient way to do that. This will be essential if you frequently cook rice.

Dry Ingredients

CORNSTARCH

A white powder derived from corn used as a slurry in many Asian stir-fries. Tip: the ratio for slurry is two parts cold water to one part cornstarch.

PANKO BREAD CRUMBS

These flaky Japanese-style bread crumbs are used in Asian cooking to create a light coating. They are high in fiber and larger than regular bread crumbs, and retain their crispness longer.

RICE FLOUR

This flour is made of ground rice. It can be used as a thickening agent or in baked goods, waffles or pancakes, producing a slightly chewier texture. When used as a bread in frying, it will produce a light and airy crust.

Fresh Ingredients

GARLIC

Garlic is part of the onion family, though more pungent than its cousins, and adds a rich flavor to any savory dish. A garlic press is handy to use on it, as it will separate the juicy pulp from the top film layer. This will get the full flavor out of the garlic.

GINGER

Ginger root has been used for thousands of years as a dietary and medicinal supplement. It has a zesty flavor and stringy texture. For baked goods, teas, candied and pickled, ginger is used in the kitchen for a variety of occasions. Pro tip: scrape the ginger with a spoon to peel off the skin; use a garlic press to remove the pulp from the stringy pith.

SCALLIONS

Scallions, often called green onions, are part of the onion family, but are milder in taste. These zesty onions can be eaten cooked or raw and make a delicious garnish.

LEMONS

This versatile citrus fruit is a popular Asian addition, and can be used in savory and sweet dishes.

VEGETABLES

Basics: onions, carrots, celery, garlic, potatoes, bundles of green scallions and a lot of ginger. My mom always had her comfort veggies: plastic bags filled with bok choy, napa cabbage and *gai-lan* (Chinese broccoli). She also made a point to add in seasonal veggies such as Swiss chard, beets and baby cherry tomatoes.

Milk

COCONUT MILK

This creamy white liquid made from the flesh of coconuts is usually packed in a can. It is great for soups, braising meats, curry and desserts.

CONDENSED MILK

This is made from removing water from cow's milk and adding sugar. This syrupy liquid can substitute for sugar in coffee and teas and is also called for in desserts.

Pots & Pans

LARGE SOUP POTS

No kitchen can function without these. For stews, soups and just about any other thing you may want to boil, these are your friends.

SAUCE PANS

It's best to keep several different sizes of pans. Choose the appropriate size according to the size of your meal so the heat will not be wasted in extra space. Great to use for heating up soups, cooking individual ramen and making sauces and gravies.

SAUTÉ PANS

Sauté pans are great for making fried eggs, sautéing and making one-pan meals.

STAINLESS-STEEL STEAMER

Steaming is a good oil-free preparation method that retains the food's nutrients. Vegetables, meat patties, frozen breads (baos) and dumplings can all be thrown in the steamer.

WOK

No Asian kitchen is complete without a wok. In fact, my mom rarely used a sauté pan. She made eggs, vegetables and sometimes even stewed meats using the wok.

Protein

CHICKEN DRUMSTICKS

The leg is a flavorful cut of dark meat. It is commonly used in Chinese braised dishes.

EGGS

Eggs are perhaps the most versatile of all proteins. Eggs are easy to prepare as a stand-alone meal, and the list of dishes that call for eggs is endless. It's a good idea to keep a dozen eggs in the fridge to have at the ready.

GROUND MEATS

Any type of ground meat, including chicken, turkey, pork and beef.

OXTAIL/BEEF SHANKS

Oxtail is the tail of the cow and beef shanks are a portion of the leg. These meats, when slow-cooked, produce the most tender and buttery textures. Wonderful to use in stews and soups.

PORK SHOULDER

You can use this for a roast, in chunks for stews and soups, sliced and cooked in a stir-fry or slow-cooked for pulled pork or carnitas. Pork shoulder is magical.

PRESERVED EGGS

These eggs are soaked in a saline solution made of ash, salt, quicklime and rice hull. This produces a creamy yolk center and turns the egg white into black jelly. It is commonly served in jook (Chinese porridge).

TOFU

Tofu is made from curds of soymilk and shaped into a block. It can be bought in different textures, soft and firm. Its flavor is bland on its own but it easily absorbs other flavors.

SPAM

This is canned cooked pork, a good option to have on hand for an addition to quick meals.

Rice & Noodles

DRIED NOODLES

Wheat, buckwheat, egg, soba and vermicelli noodles are just some of the noodles handy to have in the pantry. With these noodles you can whip up fast noodle dishes any night of the week.

INSTANT NOODLES

This packaged noodle block has already been dried and precooked. Great for those quick 10-minute meals. They can be enhanced with egg, Spam or spinach.

JASMINE RICE

This long-grain white rice has a floral aroma. A sack of jasmine rice is a must for your pantry. A rice cooker comes highly recommended to make your rice dish most convenient.

Sauce, Oil & Wine

BLACK BEAN SAUCE

This fermented black soybean paste is used in stir-fries and other braised dishes in Asian cooking.

FISH SAUCE

This is a briny liquid often made from fermented anchovies and salt used in many Southeast Asian dishes. Its pungent flavor adds a level of depth and complexity to any dish. A little goes a long way.

GOCHUJANG

This Korean fermented chili sauce has a thick, sticky texture. It's spicy and slightly sweet in flavor.

HOISIN SAUCE

This is a thick, sweet and tangy sauce made from fermented soybeans, garlic, five spices, sugar and sesame oil.

KETCHUP

One of America's favorite condiments, this sweet and tangy sauce is made from tomatoes, vinegar, sugar and other seasonings. It's great to use in sauces, marinades or just for dipping.

RED WINE

Used in a braising liquid or in a goblet with dinner, either choice provides an extra zing to your night.

OYSTER SAUCE

Used to strengthen the flavor of a dish, this dark sauce is made from oyster extracts. There are many variations of oyster sauce, varying in sweetness and added caramel for color. The highest quality is naturally dark and does not contain caramel.

RICE WINE VINEGAR

This acidic yet sweet vinegar is made by fermenting sugar in rice. It is great to use in dressings, as a pickling liquid or in stir-fries.

SESAME OIL

This oil is derived from sesame seeds and has a roasted and nutty flavor. It is used in many marinades and garnishes.

SOY SAUCE

Liquid flavoring made of fermented soybeans used to enhance many Asian dishes.

TOMATO PASTE

This thick paste is great to add tomato flavor into soups and as a braising for meat.

VEGETABLE COOKING OIL

This oil—extracted from seeds, fruit, grains and nuts—is the preferred oil in Chinese cooking. It has a high cooking point that is great for all stir-fries, meats and noodles.

XIAOXING RICE WINE

This wine made from fermented rice is commonly used in Chinese cooking. It is perfect for marinating meat and fish, or as a braising liquid. It is the Eastern version of a dry sherry.

Spices & Seasoning

CHICKEN BOUILLON

These hardened cubes are made from chicken stock. They are perfect for making a flavorful soup broth or to add to any sauce.

CHINESE FIVE-SPICE POWDER

This powder is used in many Chinese dishes, particularly as a meat seasoning. The powder blend consists of clove, cinnamon, fennel, star anise and Szechuan peppercorn.

CHINESE HERBS AND TEAS

Dried goji berries, jujubes (dried red dates), wood ear, snow fungus, adzuki red beans—these are just a few of the roots, fungus and herbs used in Chinese medicine and the household as well. Chinese teas offer health benefits such as a healthier immune system and lower cholesterol. The tea leaf itself is a staple. There are a handful of different types of tea leaves (black, green, oolong, pu-erh, white, yellow, to name a few), which come in dozens of varieties and styles to make the art of tea drinking a unique and salubrious experience every time.

GROUND WHITE PEPPER

While made from the same plant, the ripeness and fermentation process of the white pepper berry makes it milder than black pepper. White pepper is used in many Chinese soups, marinades and stir-fries, and is a spice alternative for dishes lighter in color in which flakes are not desirable.

RED PEPPER FLAKES

These dried spicy pepper flakes and seeds are great for garnishes to any spice lover's savory dishes. They are also the main ingredient used to make chili oil.

STAR ANISE PODS

This brown pod shaped like a star is the fruit from the evergreen tree (*illicium verum*). It has a strong licorice flavor and should be used in small quantities in your savory dishes. Whole or ground, it can be used to flavor anything from cocktails and drinks to baked goods, ground meat and pasta sauce.

TABLE SALT

While salty is one of the five basic tastes, salt is the world's most popular ingredient. A flavor highlighter and suppressor, salt comes in many different forms for different purposes. Refined table salt is the most common type, and is infused with iodine, an essential mineral that supports metabolism and other functions.

Sweeteners

BROWN SUGAR

Brown sugar is made by adding molasses to white sugar. Brown sugar creates a softer, chewier texture in baked goods than white sugar. Although commonly used in sweets, brown sugar can also be used on baked carrots, ham, sweet potatoes, yams and squash.

HONEY

Honey is a naturally occurring sweetener that can be used topically for burns and infections, as well as a dietary supplement. In addition to sweetening desserts and drinks, it can also be used in meat marinades.

ROCK SUGAR

Less sweet than granulated sugar, rock sugar is unprocessed in crystallized form that comes in small cubes or in irregular shapes. It is used in both sweet and savory Chinese dishes.

Utensils & Tools

BOWLS AND PLATES

Keep a collection of plates and bowls of different widths. Choose the appropriate size depending on what you plan to serve. Whether you are serving soup, salad or peanuts, the container should fit the dish. (Note: bowls are more commonly used than plates in Chinese culture.)

CHOPPING BOARD

Keep a couple of cutting boards on hand for different foods: one for cutting raw meats and other strong foods such as onions, and another for fruit and vegetables.

CLEAVER

This knife has a heavy, broad blade. It can hack through bones and whack large vegetables, yet is sharp enough to cut food delicately. I don't remember having too many knives growing up since the cleavers did it all.

COLANDER

Use this to rinse vegetables and drain the hot water from the boiling noodles.

FOIL

Great for lining dishes that are going into the oven as it ensures easy cleanup. Cover dishes to keep the food warm.

KITCHEN SHEARS

These are used to cut through chicken bones and other tough foods, and for trimming vegetables.

LADLE

An essential utensil scooping out large amounts of liquids.

LONG CHOPSTICKS

These can be used as a whisks, spatulas and eating utensils. Although used throughout Asia, Chinese chopsticks specifically are longer and thicker than those in other countries (about 25 centimeters). Proper use of chopsticks is to hold them in the middle. Hold the bottom stick between the tip of your ring finger and the hollow between your index and thumb. Keep your ring finger straight. Place the other stick on top, between your thumb, index and middle fingers. The bottom stick should remain stationary, while the top will maneuver to pick up your food.

MASON JARS FOR CONDIMENTS

These glass jars are great for pickling and storing leftovers. They can be stacked to maximize fridge space.

METAL SPATULA

This is an essential tool for stirring and flipping foods.

RICE PADDLE

Use this to scoop out the rice from the rice cooker.

ACKNOWLEDGMENTS

Thank you to my mom, who may not be remembered for being a chef, but is/was a caring woman who was determined to feed her family. You sparked my fire of needing to create in the kitchen. Thank you to both my grandmothers, who are the strongest and most resourceful women I know, who have lived through so many of the struggles of the human experience.

This book never would have been possible if I had not crossed paths with Hannah and Julianne. Hannah, you provided the visual piece needed so that I could share my ideas with others. You worked tirelessly to get us organized and often hurt your back from constantly bending for each food shoot. Julianne, you extracted and scraped every bit of the bone so that I would be able to tell my story. Thank you to Kelsey for testing the recipes and helping to format them. Thank you to Gail for her insight in making sure that the overall book made sense from page to page.

Thank you to all the people who provided opportunities and dreamed for me when I didn't have the dream myself. I want to be that same catalyst for making others' dreams a reality. Thank you to Tom Nyugen, my counselor at De Anza College who recognized my determination and heart. Thank you to my mentor, Francis Kong, who initially helped me realize that food was a recurring theme in my life and gave me a platform to share my story. Thank you to all of the surrogate mothers who have nurtured me and helped me become who I am today. The contributions you have made in my life are invaluable.

INDEX

ABOUT THE AUTHOR

Samantha Mui is a native of the California Bay Area. A former culinary student and current food blogger, she has worked in and out of the food industry for more than a decade. Her cooking style is inspired by her travels abroad where she has experienced culture through cuisine. She has been a guest on the Bay Area TV show *Check, Please!* You can see what she's cooking up on her blog and elsewhere.

INSTAGRAM

@sammyeats

FACEBOOK

facebook.com/samantha.mui.58

BLOG

samtillymui.wordpress.com

"*Melting Pot* is an enchanting story of food and recipes that showcases Mui's unique journey and transformation from the child of immigrant parents into a strong culinary artist. Using accessible ingredients and simple techniques, Mui recreates dishes that are packed with flavors reminiscent of home, and can be replicated in any home cook's kitchen. It's a book I'll be keeping on my kitchen shelf."

—GRACE KEH, author of *Food Lovers' Guide to San Francisco*

"*Melting Pot* isn't just a cookbook—it's a heartfelt, delicious journey and coming together of East and West guided by Mui's warm, authentic, and relatable voice. You will magically be transported from the page into Mui's kitchen and guided on a wonderful culinary journey to feed your stomach and soul. A delightful read you will want to devour cover to cover!"

—DION LIM, anchor-reporter at ABC7 in San Francisco and author of *Make Your Moment*

CPSIA information can be obtained
at www.ICGtesting.com
Printed in the USA
BVHW021033210820
586985BV00022B/396